PHOTOSHOP CS3
Photo Effects Cookbook

PHOTOSHOP CS3
Photo Effects Cookbook

Tim Shelbourne

O'REILLY®

First edition for the United States, its territories and dependencies,
Central and South America, and Canada, published in 2007 by O'Reilly Media, Inc.

O'Reilly Media, Inc.
1005 Gravenstein Highway North
Sebastopol, CA 95472
USA
www.oreilly.com

Editorial Director: *Edie Freedman, O'Reilly Media*
Cover Designer: *Edie Freedman, O'Reilly Media*

O'Reilly books may be purchased for educational, business, or sales promotional use.
For more information, contact our corporate/institutional sales department:
(800) 998-9938 or corporate@oreilly.com

Downloadable image files of the examples in this book can be found online at:
http://examples.oreilly.com/9780596515041

International Standard Book No. 0-596-51504-9
ISBN-13: 978-0-596515-04-1

This book was conceived by:
ILEX, Lewes, England
www.ilex-press.com

ILEX Editorial:
Publisher: *Alastair Campbell*
Creative Director: *Peter Bridgewater*
Editorial Director: *Tom Mugridge*
Editor: *Chris Gatcum*
Art Director: *Julie Weir*
Designer: *Ginny Zeal*

Manufactured in China

9 8 7 6 5 4 3 2 1

Contents

READY TO COOK?

THE INGREDIENTS

INTRODUCTION

This is a cookbook with a difference. To follow these recipes you'll require no perishable goods and there's no slaving over a hot stove. Adobe Photoshop is your virtual kitchen and the only ingredients you'll need are your own creative talent and enthusiasm. The analogy with cooking is really more accurate than it would at first seem. The mix of the ingredients and garnishes in Photoshop present the digital creative with a myriad of digital imaging cordon-bleu dishes.

Essentially, nothing is impossible with Photoshop as your chosen digital imaging application; reality can be turned on its head, and you can perform digital alchemy. Day can be turned to night, skin can be transformed to wood or stone, and that image of your pet dog can sport a knowing, but subtle grin. If your experience of digital image manipulation so far consists of simple tonal adjustments and color correction, then you're in for a few treats as you read through the following pages. If you're a more advanced Photoshop user, there's a wealth of techniques you can add to your Photoshop armoury. Like any other recipe book, the *Photoshop CS3 Photo Effects Cookbook* is an invaluable resource that you'll return to again and again, and it's a real bonus for those times when inspiration runs short or you need to pin down a particular effect. The book is organized into sections, each covering a particular genre of Photoshop recipes, allowing you to easily find anything from simulating rain to cooking up the look of stunningly realistic oil paintings.

There are a number of key skills and specific tools that are used a lot throughout the book, so this 'Ready To Cook' section is a great place to familiarize yourself with—or to refresh you knowledge of—the basic ingredients.

So, rattle those virtual pots and pans and cook up a storm with the *Photoshop CS3 Photo Effects Cookbook...*

The are a host of improvements to the way Photoshop looks and works in version CS3, and here we're going to take a quick look at a selection of the most significant ones. Throughout this edition of the *Photoshop CS3 Photo Effects Cookbook*, you'll see projects that feature many of these new and improved image editing techniques. This starts with the very first exercise—Creative Black and White—where we'll use the new CS3 Black & White command instead of the old Channel Mixer. So, if you thought you knew Photoshop, read on! There's a whole new world just a few clicks away.

SMART OBJECTS

Smart Objects are something really quite special in Photoshop CS3. Normally, when you transform a layer, Photoshop resamples the image information, which can be quite destructive in terms of image quality, especially if you transform the layer more than once. Smart Objects prevent this from happening by preserving the integrity of the original source image. In effect, a Smart Object is a special kind of layer.

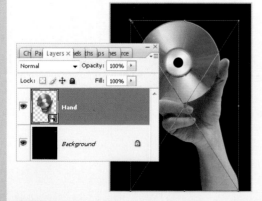

There is one important point about Smart Objects that's worth bearing in mind: you can't perform any operations that change the pixels on a Smart Object layer, such as painting, dodging, or burning. To do this, you have to first right-click the Smart Object layer and choose Rasterize Layer to convert it back to a conventional layer.

SMART FILTERS

Using any Photoshop filter as a Smart Filter has huge advantages over using the "non-smart" filters in earlier versions of Photoshop. In these earlier versions, if you used a filter such as Gaussian Blur, its effect was set in stone once you hit OK in the filter dialog. Smart Filters have changed all that! By using Smart Filters in CS3 (by going to **Filter** > **Convert For Smart Filters**), you can re-adjust the strength or settings within the filter as many times as you like. When it's converted for Smart Filters, you'll see the layer has a symbol attached to its thumbnail. You can then activate any of the filters via the Filter menu and apply them to the layer as Smart Filters. Once you click OK within the Filter dialog you'll see an entry for that particular filter associated with the Smart Filters layer in the Layers palette. By double-clicking this filter entry, you can edit the filter and apply different settings via the same filter dialog.

Smart Filters are also supplied with their own layer masks; by painting on a mask, you can selectively hide the effect of the filter. You can apply as many Smart Filters as you like to a layer—each one will be stacked on top of any existing Smart Filters, each with its own entry.

MULTIPLE CLONE SOURCES

In earlier versions of Photoshop, you could use the Clone Stamp tool or the Healing tool to clone from one document to another, or one layer to another. Cloning is an invaluable tool for image restoration and retouching, but has been much improved in CS3, as you can now set multiple clone sources. This magic happens thanks to the Clone Source palette (**Window > Clone Source**). But there is more to the Clone Source palette than just that. Thanks to this new cloning wizardry, you can now see a semi-opaque overlay of the source you're cloning from on the image you're cloning over. Not only that, but you can even scale and rotate your clone source image on the target document. You can even choose different blending modes for the Clone Source preview, which can help you accurately position and place the cloned object.

9

CS3 IMPROVEMENTS

REFINE EDGES

Once you've made a selection, you'll often want to change it in some way, such as soften its edges. This facility, and a whole host of others, is accessible via the new Refine Edges command in Photoshop CS3. All of the options in the Refine Edges dialog affect the edge of the selection in one way or another.

The available options are:

Radius: This slider controls the width of the boundary around the edge of the selection in which any of the other edge refinements do their work.

Contrast: This slider sharpens the selection edge, which is useful on images with lots of image artifacts, or where the selection edge seems a little fuzzy.

Smooth: Sometimes the edge of a selection will be a little jagged, but this slider holds the solution. As the name suggests, this option will smooth the selection edge. The range is from 1 to 100; a small value smoothes the edge a little, while higher values increase the effect.

Feather: This option, which used to be a completely independent command in earlier versions of Photoshop, softens the transition between the edge of the selection and the surrounding pixels, hence giving a "feathered" appearance to the edge. You can enter a range of between 0 and 250 pixels here.

Contract/Expand: These options shrink or expand the selection, respectively. You can use a value of between 0-100% for each option.

NEW, IMPROVED CURVES

The Curves command is something we use quite a lot throughout the recipes in this book. In previous versions of Photoshop, the use of the Curves dialog could be a pretty hit-and-miss affair for the Photoshop novice, but in CS3 there have been significant improvements to the dialog itself and the way the Curves command works. Not least of these improvements is the fact that the dialog window is now twice the size it used to be, which makes working with a curve much easier. One of the biggest CS3 Curves improvements is the addition of curve presets, which can make your image editing much easier and more predictable. Rather than dragging a curve to the appropriate shape yourself, you can now choose a wide range of commonly used curves from the preset box, such as Increase Contrast, Color Negative, Darker, and Lighter, among others. Of course, you can still make your own curve manually, but you can now save it as a preset along with all of the supplied ones. The new dialog also features a histogram overlay, so you can see the distribution of tones throughout the image as you work.The Curves command is an invaluable tool for tweaking exposure and tone of your images, and in CS3 it's now even better!

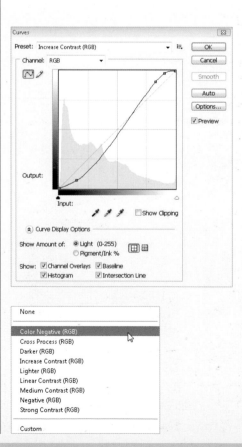

QUICK SELECTION TOOL

All of the selection tools have their own strengths and weaknesses when it comes to making selections, but there is a new selection tool in Photoshop CS3 that deserves special attention. The Quick Selection tool is a giant leap forward in Photoshop terms and, as the name suggests, it enables you to make complicated selections very quickly and puts all other selection tools in the shade when it comes to ease of use. Its strength lies in the tool's ability to select objects simply by "painting" over them with the tool. It's actually best if you do this little by little, changing the size of the selection "brush" to suit the size and shape of the area you're selecting. Often the accuracy of the selection is very good indeed, but the tool can be made even more accurate by activating the Auto Enhance option in the Options bar. Of course, you're still not going to get a super-accurate selection every time, and the Quick Selection tool can often select areas that you don't want included. But even this situation is quickly resolved; once your selection has been made, you can hold down the Alt/Opt key and paint with the tool to subtract unwanted areas from the active selection. There's even an option to sample from all layers when making your chosen selection.

10

The ability to make accurate selections is key to the art of successful image manipulation. Selections are the means by which you let Photoshop know which parts of a particular image or layer it should copy, manipulate, or apply a particular filter or effect to. Active selections are indicated by a "marquee;" an animated dotted line also referred to as "marching ants." Photoshop has many ways of enabling the creation of selections, although, strictly speaking, these fall into two distinct categories. The Marquee tools are located in the Toolbox and consist of:

Lasso tool: Used for making arbitrary, freehand selections.

Polygonal Lasso tool: Used for freehand selections by constructing polygonal (straight-sided) shapes; useful for selecting geometrically-shaped elements within an image.

Magnetic Lasso tool: This tool attempts to "snap" to high-contrast edges within an image. Its magnetic qualities can be adjusted via the settings in the Tool Options bar.

Above this nest of selection tools are the geometric marquee tools. These consist of Rectangular and Elliptical marquee tools, and Single Row and Single Column selection options. Although these geometric selection tools might seem to be of minimal use, they are often used throughout the image manipulation process—for creating borders and vignettes in particular. The edges of all of the selections made with these tools—and indeed the edges of any active selection—can be feathered, using the Feather value in the Options bar to create softer transitions between selected and unselected areas.

The Magic Wand deserves special attention, and is a tool you will come to appreciate more and more as your Photoshop confidence and ability increases. With this tool, you can instruct Photoshop to select areas of a similar color or tone within an image. These areas of color can be contiguous (joined) or non-contiguous (located in different parts of the image). The wand works on a tolerance principle, which dictates how close in tone or color two or more pixels must be before they are both selected with a single click of the Magic Wand. The wand can be set to make a selection from the current layer, or from all visible layers within the image. After setting the tolerance and options for the wand, selections are made by simply clicking the color or tone that you wish to select.

OTHER SELECTION TECHNIQUES

There are a couple of other methods for making selections that, although not accessible from the Toolbox, are still vitally important when it comes to making accurate selections.

Quick Mask is a great method for creating complex selections and fine-tuning them. You enter Quick Mask mode using the icon at the base of the Toolbox, or by

hitting Q on the keyboard. Once the mode is entered, you can make a complex selection by painting onto the mask, using the Brush tool. Painting with black as the foreground color applies the mask, and painting with white erases it. Varying shades of gray make the resulting selection semi-transparent. So, in Quick Mask mode, you paint over the parts of the image you want to select, exiting Quick Mask mode when you have completed the painting to reveal the marching ant selection.

A less labor-intensive selection method is Photoshop CS3's new Quick Selection tool, which nests with the Magic Wand tool in the Toolbar. The Quick Selection tool is incredibly easy to use, and lets you make complex selections very quickly. Simply paint over the objects you wish to select and let Photoshop do the rest.

The final selection method that warrants a mention is Color Range, accessed through **Select > Color Range**. Begin by choosing the Eyedropper tool from the Toolbar and sampling the color or tone you wish to select from the image itself. Within the dialog, select "Sampled Colors" from the Range box. The Fuzziness slider within the dialog is similar in function to the Tolerance setting used for the Magic Wand and lets you dictate the tolerances used by Photoshop when deciding how close together two or more colors or tones need to be before they should both be selected.

The Color Range dialog also gives you the useful option of applying a black or white matte to your image so it is clear which parts of the picture will be selected when you click the OK button.

WORKING WITH LAYERS

Layers are the bedrock of successful image editing in Photoshop. You can imagine Photoshop layers as separate sheets of clear acetate, hovering over your background image. By using layers it's possible to make all manner of changes to the picture, without affecting one single pixel on the original background image.

When you open a digital image in Photoshop, it contains only one layer; the Background layer. In Photoshop, layers are held in the Layers palette and stack one on top of the other. Whenever you copy and paste image data into a file in Photoshop, the new image component is placed on its own separate layer, which you can move, edit, manipulate, and resize to your heart's content. The usefulness of layers does not stop there; each layer can interact with the ones below it in the Layers palette, via blending modes, providing almost unlimited creative possibilities.

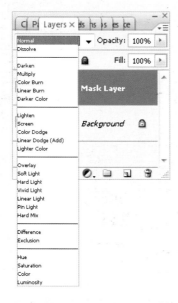

Add to this the fact that the opacity of a layer can be modified between fully opaque and semi-transparent, and it's easy to see why layers are so important to digital image manipulation.

Layers can also be moved and resized independently of each other. The key to moving layers is the Move tool. This tool, located in the top right of the Toolbar, can be used to drag an entire layer—and consequently the image elements on that layer—into a new position within the image. This repositioning can be on a grand scale (from one side of the image to the other) or you can move the layer a pixel at a time, using the arrow keys on the keyboard.

You can also scale or distort layers using the **Edit > Transform** menu. Once you have selected one of the layer-transforming options, the image elements on the target layer are enclosed by a transform bounding box; the size and shape of the layer can be adjusted by dragging any of the handles placed around the edge of the box.

One of the most basic ways to create a new layer is to create a duplicate layer. A duplicate layer is an exact duplicate of the original layer. To make a duplicate layer, simply right-click the layer you wish to make the duplicate

from and choose **Layer > Duplicate Layer** (or hit Ctrl/Cmd+J on the keyboard). This can be a tremendously useful device in many areas of image editing. As a simple example, a moderately underexposed digital camera image can be easily corrected by making a duplicate copy layer and setting the new layer's blending mode to Screen.

STACKING ORDER OF LAYERS

Layers can be stacked in any order in the Layers palette, with the exception of the original Background layer, which is always fixed in position at the bottom of the stack. The layers can be moved up and down the layer stack by clicking and dragging them. Their new location in the layer stack is indicated by a highlight in the Layers palette.

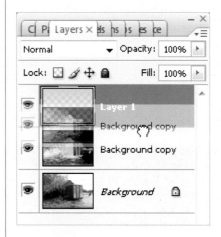

There are some types of layers which are completely blank and contain no image data whatsoever, but still have a marked effect on lower layers and on the image as a whole. These "adjustment layers" make global color or tonal changes to the image which can be readjusted throughout the editing process, or subtle color fills, textures, or patterns can be applied, with no permanent effect on the original Background image layer.

To save an image that has multiple layers, it should be saved in Photoshop's native file format (.PSD), although, in some cases, layers can be saved in a TIFF file. If you want to save the finished image as a JPEG or TIFF file, it's best to flatten the layered file before saving it, unless you have a specific use that demands otherwise. When you flatten a layered file in Photoshop, you are merging all of the layers together into a single un-layered image. It's worth noting that once an image is flattened, the layers are no longer editable, so you must make sure that you have definitely finished working on the separate layers before flattening. To flatten the layers in an image, go to **Layer > Flatten Image**.

12

LAYER MASKS

So you have a number of layers in the Layers palette, and all of these combine to create the whole image; but what if you want to partially obscure or hide just a part of a particular layer? You could simply use the Eraser tool to erase part of the layer, but this action is frighteningly permanent and there's no going back once the erasing is done. This is where layer masks come to the rescue!

Layer masks are so called because they literally mask out part of a layer. A layer mask is associated with and linked to an existing image layer. These masks work on a grayscale principle, where black hides the image layer and white makes it visible. To add a layer mask, first choose the layer you want to apply it to in the Layers palette, then click the Add Layer Mask icon at the base of the palette. You can paint onto a mask with any of the painting and drawing tools in the Toolbox, or you can construct shapes within the mask by making and filling selections.

By using various shades of gray in the mask, you can very accurately control the transparency of the associated image layer. The image above shows a layer mask in its simplest form, which creates a simple vignette effect. The grayscale contents of a layer mask can be blurred or have any number of filters and gradients applied to it, for an almost infinite array of incredible effects. You can also view and modify layer masks in isolation. Simply Alt/Opt-click the thumbnail of the layer mask in the Layers palette to view the mask in its pure grayscale form.

TYPE LAYERS

To add type (or text) to an image, choose the Horizontal or Vertical Type tool from the Toolbar. With the Type tool active, click within your image. A new layer with a large "T" (indicating a Type layer) will appear in the Layers palette, and a flashing cursor appears on screen, indicating that you can now type your text via the keyboard.

When you add type or text to an image, the type is automatically placed on a new layer of its own (indicated by a large "T" symbol in the Layers palette). A type layer is a special kind of layer, wholly separate from the other pixel-based layers in an image that contains photographic elements. This allows the type to be re-edited at any point, and the font and size can be modified. The size, type face, and color used for the type can be chosen and modified from the Options bar in Photoshop. Once your type has been edited fully and you're happy with the result, the type layer can be rasterized to convert the vector shapes to pixels. Once rasterized, the type layer can be modified and manipulated in just the same way as any other pixel-based elements, so you can blur or apply filters. Just one word of warning here; if you need to rasterize a type layer (to convert it to a standard pixel layer), the type will no longer be editable.

After typing the text, you can edit it using the Options bar—after clicking and dragging over the type to highlight it. You can move type anywhere within the image by simply clicking and dragging anywhere on the screen outside of the actual type area. Once you're happy with the appearance of the type, make sure to click the Commit tick in the Options bar.

For as long as it remains on its own layer, you can re-edit the type at any time by double-clicking the thumbnail for the type layer in the Layers palette.

In addition to the standard horizontal and vertical Type tools are the Type Mask tools, nested in the Toolbar. These can be very useful, but differ from the standard versions as they make a selection based on your chosen font face, rather than adding solid type. You can then paint within the type mask selection, or even fill it with another image. The Type Mask tools do not generate a type layer in the Layers palette; they simply make a selection which can be active on any layer you choose.

13

WORKING WITH LAYERS

LAYER STYLES

Layer styles decorate and enhance layers, and are a powerful weapon in your fight against boring digital images. As the name suggests, layer styles are applied only to layers, and more particularly, they are only applied to the visible elements within the target layer. You can add a layer style to a layer by clicking the ● symbol at the base of the Layers palette.

One of the most frequently used layer styles is Drop Shadow, which, when used subtly, can add depth and realism to an image. Once a style is chosen from the list, Photoshop displays a dialog box that contains a comprehensive selection of properties that you can modify and fine-tune.

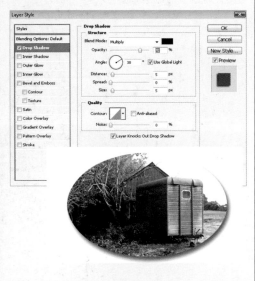

Individual layer styles can be combined together on a single layer, and remain editable for as long as the attached layer is visible in the Layers palette.

More varied and unusual layer styles can be found in the Styles palette, opened using **Window > Styles**.

These are packaged combinations of layer styles, fills, and textures that can be used to create particular surface and texture effects. In addition to the default styles, additional style sets can be loaded, each of which relates to a particular use.

To re-edit a layer style, simply double-click the effects pane attached to the layer to call up the dialog box.

| Reset Styles... |
| Load Styles... |
| Save Styles... |
| Replace Styles... |
| Abstract Styles |
| Buttons |
| Dotted Strokes |
| Glass Buttons |
| Image Effects |
| Photographic Effects |
| Text Effects 2 |
| Text Effects |
| Textures |
| Web Styles |

GRADIENTS, PATTERNS AND FILLS

You can access special fill layers via the Layers menu (**Layer > New Fill Layer**), with options including Solid Color, Pattern, and Gradient.

A solid color layer is a layer filled with a solid color chosen from the standard Color Picker. These solid color layers are useful for providing areas of continuous tone and color across a layer, or they can be used in conjunction with layer blending modes and opacity to tint all or part of an underlying layer. Solid fill layers appear with a layer mask attached to them by default, and, as you've already seen, you can paint onto this mask to hide parts of the fill layer.

Gradient layers supply you with gradient fills, which give subtle transitions between a number of colors, or transitions between a fully opaque color and an entirely transparent layer. Photoshop has many preset gradients that can be chosen directly from the Gradient Picker.

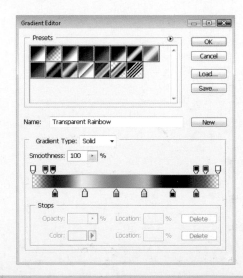

We can also apply gradients manually, using the Gradient tool. The Gradient tool is chosen from the Toolbar, and by default is nested underneath the Paint Bucket tool. If the tool is not visible in the Toolbar, simply click and hold on the Paint Bucket, and choose Gradient from the flyout.

When using the Gradient tool, placing a gradient is a simple case of clicking and dragging. The angle of the gradient is controlled by the angle at which you drag the tool. On a Gradient Fill layer, the angle is modified in the dialog box.

The simplest gradient is Foreground to Background, where Photoshop gives us a transition between the current foreground and background colors as displayed by the color swatches in the Toolbar. Another form of gradient that appears often in the recipes in this book is Foreground to Transparent. With this gradient, Photoshop supplies a transition between the current foreground color and complete transparency. This type of gradient is especially useful when used over a layer mask to seamlessly blend two separate layers:

There's another variable concerning gradients which is worth a mention—the gradient type. This determines the shape, or format, which Photoshop uses for the way the gradient is applied.

As a general rule, the linear and radial gradients are the ones we'll use most often, as these types of gradient supply the most control and versatility.

Pattern layers (accessible using **Layer > Fill Layer > Pattern**) are layers that contain patterns supplied by Photoshop. On first sight, these may seem fairly unexciting and redundant, as to a great extent we're limited by Photoshop's supplied patterns. However, there is real power in pattern layers when used in conjunction with layer blending modes. As you'll see throughout this book, pattern layers can, for instance, be used to create very realistic paper and surface textures. As with gradients, the actual patterns themselves are chosen from swatches in the Pattern Picker, and extra sets of patterns can be loaded via the small right-pointing arrow. There are many pattern libraries available, giving many creative possibilities. The actual scale of the pattern can be controlled via the scale slider, allowing you to adjust the size of your pattern in proportion with the current image it overlays.

14

Often, an image direct from a digital camera may be a little soft, and will benefit from a little judicious sharpening. Indeed, you are far better disabling any in-camera sharpening and sharpening images in Photoshop after the event, as this gives you far more control over the final degree of sharpness in the image.

Your one-stop-shop for sharpening images in Photoshop is the Unsharp Mask filter. This wonderfully powerful sharpening device is derived from an age-old printing process which improved the sharpness of an image printed from a film negative. Because its effect can be so powerful, using the Unsharp Mask filter demands some restraint, and you are far better using it subtly a couple of times rather than going for a single big hit.

One point to bear in mind is that sharpening any image should be the very last action within Photoshop before saving the final version of an image, and should be done after all other image manipulation has been completed.

The Unsharp Mask filter works by identifying the edges in an image and subtly exaggerating the contrast between the pixels which lie either side of this edge. In an unsharp image, the boundaries between these pixels are soft and indistinct. When using Unsharp Mask, you instruct Photoshop to narrow these boundaries, and, with the various controls, tell it how wide and how much contrast the boundaries need to have before the edge is sharpened by the filter. Essentially, the resulting sharpness is actually a bit of an illusion, with higher contrast between the tonal boundaries giving the appearance of a sharper image.

Using the Unsharp Mask filter itself is an inexact science. There are no hard and fast rules and no defined recipes for settings, as the individual settings required very much depend on the image you are sharpening and its end use.

There are 3 fields of variables within the filter:

Amount: This slider governs the overall extent of the sharpening effect. You can think of this slider as the sharpening volume control, as it controls how powerfully the other sliders' settings are applied to the image. It's useful to initially set this slider at a high value—say 200%—so you can easily see the effect of the settings you choose for the Radius and Threshold sliders. Then, slowly reduce the Amount value to control the severity of the sharpening effect across the entire image.

Radius: The Radius setting determines the width of the sharpening effect, or how far across the edge boundaries the sharpening effect is spread. This slider needs to be used with great care, as increasing the Radius value too much can result in ugly white halos along sharpened edges. Usually, a Radius value of 1-3 pixels will be appropriate for most images.

Threshold: With the Threshold slider, you inform Photoshop just how different in brightness two or more pixels should be before the boundary between them is considered an edge that should be sharpened. Using a very low setting will sharpen the majority of pixels within an image, while higher settings will sharpen only obviously contrasting edges. As a consequence, a higher setting here will sharpen the edges in an image but not sharpen subtle textures. This is a good way to sharpen the main edges in a portrait, such as the hair, without the unwanted and unflattering effect of sharpening the texture of the subject's skin

A good starting point for the settings in the Unsharp Mask filter is Amount 200, Radius 2, Threshold 1. Although these setting are likely to be too severe for many images, starting with these settings will make any modifications to the Radius and Threshold values more obvious.

Here we have a typical sharpening scenario:

1 Although this image is fairly sharp, there are signs of the slight softness often associated with images direct from a digital camera.

2 As discussed previously, these settings for the Unsharp Mask are a good starting point, although the results are often rather too sharp and unnatural. Although the sharpness has improved from the original image, the low Threshold value has over-sharpened the texture of the skin.

3 These settings, with the Radius value set to 10, illustrate the danger of using the Radius slider at too high a value. The skin texture is very exaggerated and ugly halos are starting to form around the edges in the image.

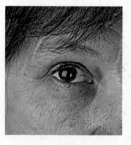

4 By setting the Radius to 2.5 and modifying the Threshold value to 4, we've achieved just about the right amount of sharpening in the right places. Skin textures are not over-emphasised, but essential edges and details are nicely sharpened. The overall degree of the effect can now be controlled with the amount slider, which I've set to 245%.

15

THE PEN TOOL, VECTORS, AND PATHS

We've already touched on vector shapes in the previous section, but it warrants a little more investigation. The vast majority of imagery in Photoshop is pixel-based. Every single digital camera image, scan, or brush stroke is made up of millions of individual pixels. Pixels exist with the sole aim of rendering your photographic images flawlessly, and can collectively create incredibly subtle gradations of color and tone. The one disadvantage of pixels is that they are completely dependent on resolution to maintain detail and sharpness. Owners of low resolution digital cameras will often be surprised and disappointed to discover that the images from the camera start to disintegrate when they attempt to print them larger than the image's optimum, resolution-dependent print size. Well, here lies the Achilles Heel of the pixel; there is only so far you can enlarge a pixel-based image before the very nature of the pixels themselves become frighteningly apparent and the image begins to disintegrate into tell-tale block of color.

Vector shapes, on the other hand, are not subject to such constraints, as they are not pixel-based. Vectors are made up of paths and are thus resolution independent. A vector will print with optimum sharpness at the size of a postage stamp, and yet can be scaled up to the size of a small building with no loss of quality or sharpness. This is the exact reason why text in Photoshop is handled as vector shapes, so the type size can be increased with no loss of edge clarity.

As Photoshop is not a true vector-based program, and because the terminology is rather confusing, you can think of vectors in Photoshop simply as paths—in essence, the two things are one and the same. Paths are invaluable for cutting out and isolating very complex shapes, and can even be converted to regular Photoshop selections after they have been drawn. Your one-stop-shop for path creation in Photoshop is the Pen tool. When you draw a path with the Pen tool, you essentially plot anchor points. To plot these anchor points, you simply click with the Pen tool. Two anchor points are needed to form a path, the path itself being the line segment between the two anchors. A straight path segment is created with single click, while curved path segments (Bézier curves) require you to click and drag the tool. These curved Path segments have direction handles attached to them, which can be dragged and repositioned to change the steepness and depth of the curve. Additionally, there are two types of paths that you can create with the Pen tool: open paths and closed paths. Open paths can be stroked with any of the painting and drawing tools in Photoshop, and closed paths can be filled with solid color or a gradient.

Throughout this book, you'll find many examples of using paths to isolate objects, create smooth flowing lines, and make selections.

Paths are stored in the Paths palette, which sits behind the Layers palette in the Photoshop workspace.

Your current path, known as the Work Path, is stored in this palette. Individual paths can be saved, to be used again later in the image editing process, by naming them in the palette itself. Generating a selection for a very complicated shape is often best achieved by this method, first drawing a path around the shape with the Pen tool.

1 This simple closed path is made with four simple clicks, giving us 4 straight path segments. It is called the current Work Path in the Paths palette:

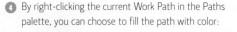

2 Here's a path made up of curved path segments, which are made by clicking and dragging with the Pen tool.

Here, you can see the direction handles that are attached to each of the curved anchor points in the path.

They can be moved to adjust each curve by holding down the Ctrl key on the keyboard and dragging one of the direction handles.

3 Here, the path is made up of both curved and straight path segments. You can see that the curved segments are indicated by the presence of the direction handles.

4 By right-clicking the current Work Path in the Paths palette, you can choose to fill the path with color:

stroke the outline of the path:

or convert it to a selection:

Tip

Remember - although paths are visible on-screen, they won't print unless you fill them with color or stroke them.

Throughout this book, you'll often use Photoshop's Lighting Effects filter (accessed using **Filter** > **Render** > **Lighting Effects**). With this filter, you can create some incredibly realistic lighting effects with just a few simple clicks. It's hard to overestimate the usefulness of this filter, which can be used for everything from creating convincing textures to adding realistic studio lighting to a portrait. You can also use alpha channels in conjunction with this filter to provide detailed and accurate texture maps, which control how the light falls and interacts with a virtual surface. You'll see some examples of this technique in the Textures section of this book.

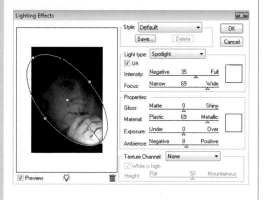

The Lighting Effects filter is surprisingly easy to use. In the Preview pane of the filter dialog, the pool of virtual light is indicated by an elliptical outline with handles anchored to it. With these handles, you can rotate and expand the light pool in any direction, simply by clicking and dragging. Various preset lighting styles can be chosen from the Style box, where you can select many different types, colors, and combinations of lights.

Once a light preset has been selected, the various sliders in the dialog can be used to modify every aspect of the light and the way it interacts with the actual image. We can control the intensity of the light—increasing it from a very gentle glow to a powerful blast of light—and we can also control how the imagined surface of the image reacts with that light, either simulating the effect of a shiny, reflective surface, or one which is completely matte. You'll be given the exact settings for these sliders whenever we use the filter in this book, but it's worth experimenting with the various options to see how you can modify, or perhaps even improve, the effects to suit your own work.

Alpha channels, used as textures within the filter, can be loaded via the Texture Channel box in the filter dialog. Again, we'll cover their specific use in throughout the book, but essentially the principles of texture channels are easy to grasp. An alpha channel—when used with the lighting filter—is a grayscale image created as an extra channel in the Channels palette in Photoshop. So, how does the Lighting Effects filter use this to simulate texture? Basically, in the alpha channel, or, to be more precise, the texture channel, white areas within the channel are interpreted as high points, or peaks, on the virtual texture surface, and black areas are interpreted as low points or valleys. Here's a typical example, using a simple fill created by the Clouds filter within the texture channel itself:

① Start by creating a new document and filling it with a solid color.

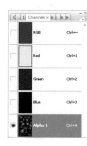

② In the Channels palette, add a new alpha channel, using the Add New Channel button at the base of the palette. Notice that the foreground and background color swatches revert to black and white, as channels can only contain shades of gray. Now, go to **Filter** > **Render** > **Clouds** to fill the channel with a clouds fill. Follow this by going to **Filter** > **Render** > **Difference Clouds** to give the fill a little more depth. We'll use this channel as our texture channel in the Lighting Effects filter.

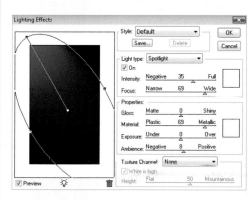

③ Return to the Layers palette and click on the filled Background layer. Start the Lighting Effects filter, using **Filter** > **Render** > **Lighting Effects**. Leaving the setting for the filter at the default values, rotate the light pool with the handles around the edges so that the light falls from top left to bottom right.

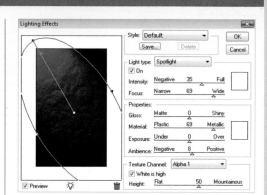

④ From the Texture Channel box, choose Alpha 1 (the cloud-filled alpha channel you just created). Notice in the Preview pane that the surface suddenly features a realistic texture, taken directly from the alpha channel. You can increase the depth of the high and low parts of the texture with the Depth slider, taking the depth scale from flat all the way up to mountainous. Click OK to apply the lighting and texture.

⑤ The completed image: from simple, flat fill to convincingly textured surface.

17

TONAL AND COLOR EFFECTS

High-key and low-key effects

As a general rule, we all aim for images that are well-balanced tonally, with a fairly equal range of light and shadow throughout. However, there are times when deliberately narrowing this tonal range can yield interesting results. For high-key images, we restrict the tonality to the upper range of the tonal scale, resulting in a soft, milky, and rather romantic effect. Low-key uses the lower end of the scale, and inspires moody and rather somber images.

The ultimate advantage of doing this with Photoshop is that we can experiment and fine-tune the effect. It is important not to confuse high-key and low-key effects with simple over- or under-exposure. In the completed images, the full tonal range should remain, but with a higher percentage of certain tones represented. Here we'll give a single image the high-key and low-key treatment to demonstrate the dramatic difference between the two effects.

High-key effect

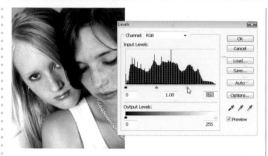

1 Open the original image in Photoshop, and go to **Image > Adjustments > Levels**. For high-key we need to restrict the majority of the tones to the upper tonal range. Begin the adjustment by moving the White Point slider below the histogram to the left. Move the slider until the input value for the white point reads 175.

2 Duplicate the background layer (Ctrl/Cmd+J) and call it "Diffuse Glow." We need to add some diffused light to the image now, so hit D on the keyboard to revert to default foreground/ background colors and go to **Filter > Distort > Diffuse Glow**. Use these settings: Graininess 9, Glow Amount 12, Clear Amount 15. Click OK and set this layer to Screen, opacity 91%.

3 The high-key look is taking shape, but the image still needs a little softening. Add a new layer (Ctrl/Cmd+Shift+N), call it "White Fill," and select the Eyedropper tool. Click with the Eyedropper in the lightest part of the faces and go to **Select > Color Range**. Use a Fuzziness slider setting of 79 and click OK.

4 With the selection active, go to **Edit > Fill**, choosing White for Contents. Blur this layer with **Filter > Blur > Gaussian Blur**. Use a Radius value of 74 pixels. Set the blending mode for this layer to Soft Light, and the opacity to 78%.

5 Flatten the image with **Layer > Flatten Image**. The few remaining dark tones in the image now need reinforcing, so choose the Burn tool from the Toolbar. In the Options bar, set the Range to Shadows and set the Exposure slider to 9%. Now, carefully use this tool over the dark tones in the image, subtly intensifying them here and there.

20

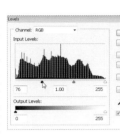

1 The technique for creating a low-key version of the image is rather different. Again, begin with the original image and go to **Image > Adjustments > Levels**. This time we need to push the tonal balance in the opposite direction. Grab the Black Point marker and drag it to the right. This will darken the shadows and the midtones. The farther to the right we drag this slider, the more dramatically low-key the final image will become.

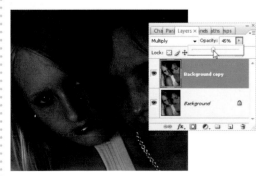

2 Pull the White Point slider a little to the left to give the highlights a bit of a boost. An input value of about 246 should do it.

3 Now, to give the image added depth, duplicate the background layer (Ctrl/Cmd+J) and go to **Image > Adjustments > Desaturate** (Ctrl/Cmd+U). Set the blending mode for this layer to Multiply and reduce the layer opacity to 45%.

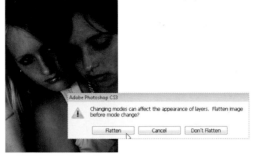

4 A low-key effect usually works best with black-and-white images, so go to **Image > Mode > Grayscale**. In the subsequent warning dialog box regarding layers, choose Flatten.

5 The image is almost complete—it just needs a little fine-tuning. This time, use the Dodge tool to lighten a few areas for added impact. Choose the Dodge tool from the Toolbar and set the Range to Midtones in the Options bar. Set the Exposure value to 10%. Use the tool on the whites of the eyes and throughout the lighter tones in the hair.

6 Increase the size of the Dodge tool with the right-facing square bracket key on the keyboard, and use it sparingly over the midtones in the girls' faces to lighten them slightly.

DODGE AND BURN

The Dodge and Burn tools in Photoshop relate to the traditional darkroom methods of making selective tonal adjustments to an image. Dodging (reducing exposure in selected areas, to lighten them) and Burning (increasing exposure, to darken them) can add real impact to lackluster black-and-white images. Both tools are subject to "Range" options, where we select Highlights, Midtones, or Shadows to determine which tones within the image will be affected. The strength, or exposure, of the tools is governed by the Exposure slider in the Tool Options. The best results are achieved by using a very low exposure setting with both tools. These tools can be used freehand, or used within a selection.

7 Change the Range for the Dodge tool to Highlights in the Options bar. Now, use this tool over a few of the lightest areas in the image. Be selective here, using the tool to enhance only the existing highlights.

Psychedelic poster effect

Every now and then, as creatives, we crave images that break away from the norm and have a bit more impact. As I've said so many times in this book, with Photoshop as your chosen tool, the possibilities for bending the rules are limitless. In this exercise, we'll take a fairly run-of-the-mill image and give it a touch of 60s Psychedelia. Here we'll replicate the effect of an iconic 60s poster, complete with halftone printing patterns. To create this image, we have to first convert it to a bitmap so that we can generate the halftone pattern. This is a very handy process that you'll find a use for over and over again.

1 First, open the start image in Photoshop and desaturate it via **Image > Mode > Grayscale**. We need to tweak the contrast a little, so go to **Image > Adjustments > Brightness/ Contrast**. Increase the Brightness to +10 and the Contrast to +38.

2 We need a halftone printing effect on the image, and we'll achieve this by converting it to Bitmap Mode. To begin that process, go to **Image > Mode > Bitmap**. In the Bitmap dialog, set the Output resolution to match the input (here it's 300 dpi), and choose Halftone Screen for Method. Click OK. In the next dialog, set the Frequency to 20 lines/inch, Angle to 45, and Shape: Round. Click OK to convert the image.

3 Now, we need to convert this file back to RGB so that we can use color on it. Go to **Image > Mode > Grayscale**, and choose 1 for Size Ratio. Then go to **Image > Mode > RGB Color**.

4 We need to change the color of the halftone print effect, and we'll do this with a Solid Color Fill Layer. Go to **Layer > New Fill Layer > Solid Color.** From the resulting Color Picker, choose an intense shade of Red. Now, change the Layer Blending Mode for this Solid Color layer to Lighten. Flatten the layers in the image via **Layer > Flatten Image**.

5 Double-click the Background Layer to make it editable, naming the layer "Main Image." Now, add another Solid Fill layer via **Layer > New Fill Layer > Solid Color**. Choose a bright Orange from the Picker and click OK. Now grab the Main Image layer in the layers palette and drag it above this orange fill layer. Now change the Blending Mode for the Main Image layer to Darken.

6 Add a new layer (Ctrl/Cmd+Shift+N), naming it "Border." Choose the Rectangular Marquee tool and drag a selection just a little way inside the outer edge of the image. Go to **Select > Inverse** so the selection makes a border around the image. Choose the Eyedropper tool and sample the red in the image. Fill this selection via **Edit > Fill**, choosing Foreground Color for Contents.

7 Now, go to **Select > Inverse** again. Click in the Foreground Color swatch and choose a bright Blue. Go to **Edit > Stroke**. Choose 20 for Stroke Width and Inside for Location. This will apply a thin line to the border around the poster. Hit Ctrl/Cmd+D to deselect.

8 Sample the Red again with the Eyedropper and select the Brush tool. Choose a hard, round brush from the Brush Picker. Paint with this brush inside the lenses in the sunglasses to make them solid red.

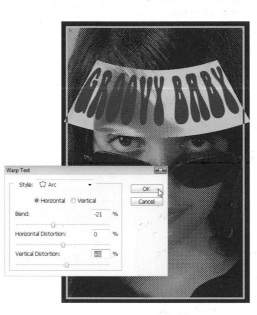

9 To add the type, choose the Horizontal Type tool. Click in the image and type your text. Here I've used a typical 60s font. Go to **Window > Character** to display the Type properties palette. From here you can adjust the Width and Height of the type. Click the Warp Text button in the Options bar. Choose Arc from the Style Box in the Warp Text dialog. Click the Horizontal radio button and adjust the Bend value to −21. Set Vertical Distortion to +8. Click OK to apply the Warp to the text.

10 Click the Commit tick in the Options Bar to apply the type. You can move the type into place with the Move tool. Finally, flatten the image via **Layer > Flatten Image**.

Creative black and white

To achieve a black and white effect in Photoshop, we can always take the route of simple desaturation or conversion to grayscale mode. However, both of these methods can lead to rather dull and uninspiring black and white images. The best monochromes have real impact, with sparkling highlights and rich, velvety dark tones. This type of monochrome image is easily created with the new Black & White command in Photoshop CS3. This command gives you the ability to alter and mix the tones in an RGB image to create truly jaw-dropping black and white images that have impact and clarity. Things may not always be as black and white as they seem!

1 When you desaturate an image or convert it to grayscale, Photoshop averages out the tones. This produces a very flat grayscale image with too little tonal latitude and a lack of contrast and visual impact.

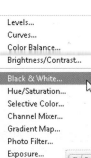

2 It's always best to use the new Black & White command via an adjustment layer. This allows more flexibility by allowing you to modify your adjustments later. Go to **Layer > New Adjustment Layer > Black & White**. Click OK in the New Layer dialog. In the Black & White dialog that opens, you'll see six sliders, each controlling a color range within the grayscale channels of the image. Be sure to check the Preview checkbox so that you can judge the effect on your image.

3 Compared to the old Channel Mixer in CS2, the Black & White command gives you much finer control over the look of your black and white image. In addition, CS3 offers useful presets; by clicking in the Preset box, you can choose from a selection of different black and white effects based on traditional photographic filters. Here we've chosen a High Contrast Red Filter.

4 In the old Channel Mixer command, knowing which sliders to adjust for a desired effect used to be rather a hit-and-miss affair. The Black & White command has a rather nifty trick up its sleeve which makes life much easier. To change the tone of a particular color range in your image, all you have to do is move your cursor outside of the dialog box, and the cursor arrow changes into the Eyedropper tool. To change the tone of the blues in the sky, simply click and hold within the sky itself and drag to adjust the nearest channel color range. You'll see the appropriate slider move as you drag.

5 You can do this anywhere in your image, targeting color and tonal ranges with pinpoint precision. Here we've darkened the blues in the sky and lightened the yellow tones in the landscape by clicking and dragging in both regions. You can see how this has altered the Yellow and Blue sliders in the Black & White dialog. The yellows have been lightened by increasing the Yellow channel and the blues have been darkened by reducing the value of the Blue channel.

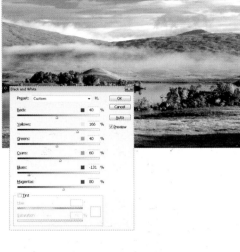

6 Of course, you can always adjust the individual sliders directly. Here we've reduced the Red, Blue, and Cyan levels and increased the Yellow for a high-contrast result.

7 You'll notice that although this is a landscape subject, the Green and Magenta sliders have little or no effect on this image. This is because these color ranges don't appear in the image itself.

Tip

TINTING BLACK AND WHITE IMAGES

One final, really useful trick you can exploit via the Black & White command. You can tint your completed image simply by checking the Tint checkbox. Choose the color from the Hue slider, then set the intensity of the tint with the Saturation slider.

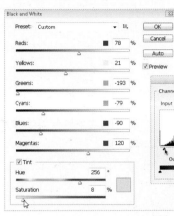

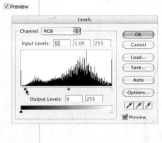

8 The goal here was to create a dark, brooding image, so we settled on this combination of color range proportions. Again, the combination depends on your personal taste, and experimentation is the key. The final settings depend on the atmosphere you're trying to create.

25

Selective coloring

Color has great power when it comes to conveying emotion and attracting attention. This power is multiplied exponentially when color is used as an accent in an otherwise monochrome image. By using selective coloring, we can draw the viewer's eye to the key areas of an image, with the colored areas adopting a jewel-like quality amid an expanse of gray.

The effect ranges from the subtle to the extreme. We can tint an image with just a hint of color, or apply an exciting splash of color to a specific area. Layer masks are an essential tool here, offering us the ability to restore color to the area of our choice, which can be controlled and restrained with the accuracy only a brush can provide.

1 The first step is to duplicate the background layer by dragging it to the new layer icon in the Layers palette or hitting Ctrl/Cmd+J.

2 Since we want most of the image to be monochrome, on this duplicate layer go to Image > Adjustments > Desaturate (Ctrl/Cmd+Shift+U). To add to the effect, give this monochrome layer a subtle blue tint. Go to Image > Adjustment > Hue and Saturation. Check the Colorize box, and move the Hue slider to 221, and the Saturation slider to 12.

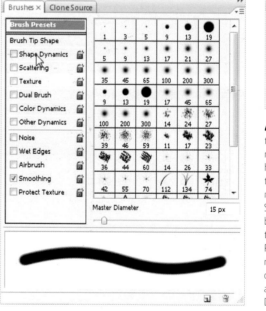

3 Now we're going to add a layer mask to the monochrome layer, which we'll use to manually restore color to parts of the image. Go to Layer > Layer Mask > Reveal All.

4 Check the Layers palette to be sure that the layer mask thumbnail is highlighted, which means that we're working on the mask, not the layer itself. Set the foreground color to black and select the Brush tool. Click in the Brush Picker and select a hard, round brush. Hit F5 to display the Brush Options and ensure that Shape Dynamics is unchecked.

Tip

LAYER MASK OR ACTUAL IMAGE LAYER?

It's very important when working with layer masks to make sure that you're painting on the mask and not on the associated image layer. There are three ways to check this:

1. Check for a bold outline around the thumbnail for the layer mask in the Layers palette.

2. Check for the mask symbol in the margin of the Layers palette (PC only). When you're working on the image layer, a Brush symbol will appear, but when you're painting on a mask, it will be replaced by a small rectangle with a circle at its center.

3. Since masks operate on a purely grayscale principle, when you're working on a layer mask, your foreground/background color swatches will always be white, black, or gray.

26

5 Paint over all of the blue and red areas on the coat and hat with black. This will hide these areas of the monochrome layer, revealing the colors on the background layer underneath. We can adjust the size of the brush as we go, using the square bracket keys on the keyboard. Zoom into the image with the Zoom tool (Z) to ensure accuracy.

6 Accuracy is all-important here, so take time to follow the edges of the colored sections very carefully. If you accidentally paint over any other part of the image, simply swap your foreground/background colors and paint over it again with white instead of black. Remember, when working on layer masks, black conceals and white reveals. Continue to paint over all of the red and blue sections.

7 Only mask out the areas of this layer that cover the red and blue sections of the costume, leaving the white areas as they are.

8 As we paint, the black areas will appear on the associated layer mask. We can check the mask by holding down the Alt/Opt key and clicking the layer mask thumbnail. This enables the actual mask to be seen in isolation.

9 We can control how vividly the colors show through the mask. Working on the mask itself, go to **Image > Adjustments > Levels**. By dragging the Black Point marker under the Output Levels bar to the right, the black tones within the layer mask are turned to gray. Where black on a layer mask is completely transparent, gray tones are only semi-transparent, which makes the revealed colors in the image layer more subtle. We can control just how subtle they are by adjusting the luminosity of the gray color on the layer mask.

Tone separations

"Soot and Snow." That's what this effect was called in the days of wet-process photography. The phrase refers to the extremes of high-contrast black and white, where all that remains of a monochrome image are the darkest darks and the lightest lights. The effect may be familiar, but used wisely it still has the potential to create some truly arresting images.

Boiling down an image to its bare essentials tonally also reduces it to its essence graphically. A creatively lit figure or portrait can be distilled into a few essential contours, taking on a hand-drawn and sometimes even abstract effect. Used alone, or as an element in a more complex photomontage, tone separation still has a certain charm.

1 To achieve the best results with this technique, it's important to begin with the right kind of image. The ideal candidate is a subject shot against a plain white background, as it already contains the element of contrast we're seeking to exaggerate.

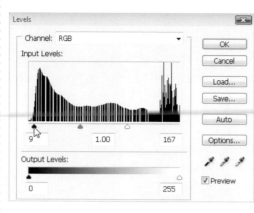

2 Duplicate the background layer by hitting Ctrl/Cmd+J on the keyboard. On the duplicate layer, go to **Image > Adjustments > Levels** to make the initial tonal adjustments. To increase the contrast, grab the White Point marker below the histogram and drag it left until the Output Levels value reads 167. Now, drag the Black Point slider to the right to a value of 9.

3 As we want a monochrome image, go to **Image > Adjustments > Desaturate** (Ctrl/ Cmd+Shift+U). Flatten the layers in the image, using **Layer > Flatten Image**.

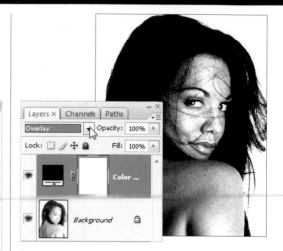

4 Hit D on the keyboard to revert to default foreground/background colors. To unify the tones in the image, click on the "Create new fill or adjustment layer" icon at the base of the Layers palette, and choose Solid Color. Click OK in the Fill Layer color picker to select black as the fill color. Set the blending mode for this layer to Overlay.

5 Return to the background layer and go to **Image > Adjustments > Brightness and Contrast**. Grab the Contrast slider and drag it up to a value of 63. This will give the remaining dark areas plenty of impact.

Tip

CHOOSING COLORS ON SOLID COLOR ADJUSTMENT LAYERS
As soon as you select Solid Color from the adjustment layer drop-down, the Color Picker opens. In the Color Picker, choose the hue you want from the vertical spectrum bar, and then select the exact shade (a combination of saturation and brightness) by clicking in the large Color Picker square. The shade is chosen by a simple click within the Picker.

6 Now we need to intensify some of the dark areas even further. Choose the Burn tool from the Toolbar and set the Exposure to 92% in the Options bar. Set the Range to Shadows. Use this tool over the eyes and lips. Increase the size of the tool with the square bracket keys on the keyboard and use it over the shadows that fall across the model's back.

9 Alternatively, we can change the white background color. Simply add another Solid Color adjustment layer and set the layer's blending mode to Darken.

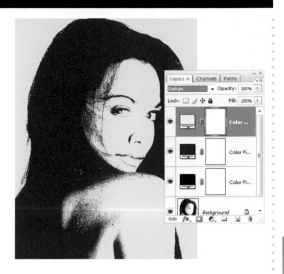

7 We need to clean up a few of the white areas in the image. Choose the Dodge tool from the Toolbar. Set the Exposure to 100% and the Range to Highlights. Use the tool to clean up the white areas. Remove any remnants of stray hairs and blemishes on the face.

8 We are not limited to having black as the main tonal color within the image. By adding another Solid Fill adjustment layer and choosing an alternative color from the picker, we can change the darker tone within the image to any color we choose.

29

GRAPHIC ART EFFECTS

Art Nouveau

Warhol screen-print

Watercolor

Oil painting

Pencil sketch

Pen-and-ink drawing

Woodcut and linocut

Art Nouveau

In Paris in the late 1880s, Art Nouveau was king. As a style, it is the very essence of all that's best in the decorative arts. To evoke the flavor of Art Nouveau in Photoshop, we can combine vector shapes with raster pixels. By using the much-maligned—and often dreaded—Pen tool, we can create a framework of lines to build upon. With the Pen tool, paths can be drawn and stroked with pressure-sensitive brushes, creating the calligraphic elegance that the Art Nouveau style requires.

Layer styles help to emboss parts of the image, giving the finished piece a decorative quality reminiscent of an illuminated manuscript. Voilà: Art Nouveau—with a digital-imaging twist!

1 With the original image open in Photoshop, go to **Filter** > **Artistic** > **Paint Daubs**. Use Brush Size 14, Sharpness 30, Brush Type Simple. This will simplify the tones in the image.

2 Now, isolate the figure from the background. Double-click the background layer to make it editable and rename it "Figure." Then hit Q on the keyboard to enter Quick Mask mode. Choose the Brush tool, and select a hard round brush from the Brush Picker. Using black as the foreground color, paint carefully over the entire figure. Remember to use the square bracket keys to alter the size of the brush, and, if you make a mistake, hit the X key to change the foreground color to white to paint out the mask. Zoom right into the flower, and, with a very fine brush, mask it out also.

3 Make sure to cover every part of the figure with the mask. Don't be too concerned about following the exact shape of the ponytail in the hair; this will be fine-tuned later. When the mask is complete, hit Q again to exit Quick Mask and generate the selection.

Now, delete the background. Depending on how the Quick Mask preference is set, either hit the Backspace key to delete the background or go to **Select** > **Inverse** (Ctrl/Cmd+Shift+I) to select the background, and then hit the Backspace key.

4 Save this selection using **Select** > **Save Selection**, and name it "Figure."

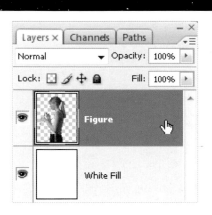

5 Hit Ctrl/Cmd+D to deselect. Add a new layer to the image (Ctrl/Cmd+Shift+N), name it "White," and go to **Edit** > **Fill** > **Use: White**. Then, grab the Figure layer in the Layers palette and drag it above the White layer.

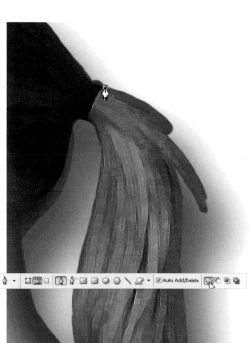

6 Add another new layer, and name it "Hair." Select the Pen tool from the Toolbar, and check to see that the Paths icon and Add To Path Area are active in the Options bar. Now, draw a path to form the decorative hair. Click with the Pen tool on the narrowest part of the ponytail nearest the girl's head. For illustrative purposes I've added a drop shadow layer style to lift the figure from the background.

7 To draw the curved paths for the hair, click and drag with the Pen tool. As we drag each curve, direction handles will appear against each curved path section. These are Bézier curves, and they can be adjusted by holding down the Alt/Opt key and moving each handle with the tool. The shape of this main hair section can be as simple or as complicated as you like, but should be made up of curves to achieve the desired result.

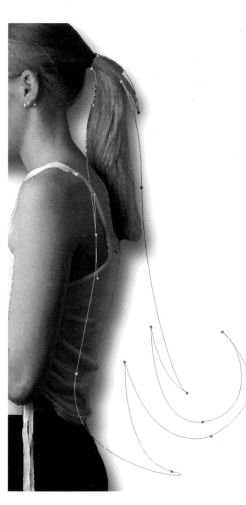

8 When we need a dramatic change of direction or a sharp point in the path, hold down the Alt/Opt key while clicking the previously plotted endpoint on the path. Work around the entire hair shape, closing the completed path by clicking again on the starting point.

9 Right-click/Ctrl-click inside the completed path and choose Make Selection; choose a Feather radius of 1 pixel. Now, click on the foreground color swatch to open the Color Picker. Select a light tan color and fill the selection, using the Paint Bucket tool.

10 Working on the hair layer, choose the Elliptical Marquee tool. Make sure that Add To Selection is active in the Options bar. Then drag a number of elliptical selections of varying sizes over the hair. Using the same foreground color, go to **Edit** > **Stroke**, choose Center for Location with a pixel width of 20. Deselect (Ctrl/Cmd+D) and drag a few smaller ellipses, stroking with a larger pixel width.

Art Nouveau continued

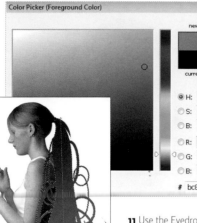

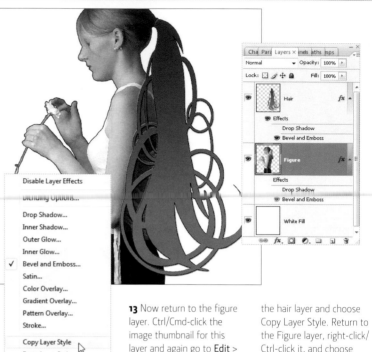

11 Use the Eyedropper tool to sample the darkest shade from the hair on the head. Then, click on the background color swatch and choose a deep russet gold. Ctrl/Cmd-click the thumbnail for the Hair layer to generate a selection.

Select the Gradient tool from the Toolbar, choose Linear Gradient, and click in the Gradient Picker to select Foreground To Background. Now click and drag a gradient from top to bottom over the hair shape.

13 Now return to the figure layer. Ctrl/Cmd-click the image thumbnail for this layer and again go to **Edit > Stroke** using a 5-pixel width. Next, right-click/Ctrl-click the hair layer and choose Copy Layer Style. Return to the Figure layer, right-click/Ctrl-click it, and choose Paste Layer Style.

12 With the selection still active, hit D to revert to default colors and go to **Edit > Stroke**, using a Stroke Width of 5 pixels. This will add an outline to the hair. Now go to **Layer > Layer Style > Bevel and Emboss**. Use these settings: Style: Emboss, Technique: Chisel Hard, Depth: 100%, Size: 5.

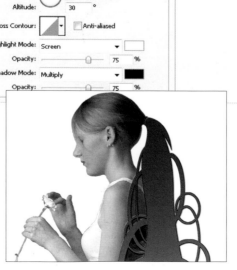

14 Still on the Figure layer, go to **Layer > New Adjustment Layer > Gradient Map**. Click on the arrow next to the Gradient Used For Grayscale Mapping box and choose Blue, Red, Yellow from the gradient swatches. Set the blending mode for this layer to Color, and reduce the opacity to 27%. This extra coloration helps to lessen the photographic qualities of the image and blends it better with the new hair.

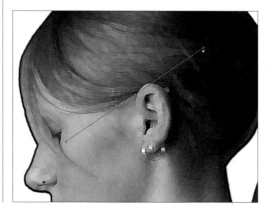

15 We'll add some line work to the image. Add a new layer (Ctrl/Cmd+Shift+N), name it "Line Work," and ensure that black is the foreground color. Click on the Brush tool and choose a small, hard-edged brush from the picker. Then select the Pen tool, and click on the tab at the top of the Layers palette to reveal the Paths palette. Draw a single curved path, following one of the edges of the hair.

34

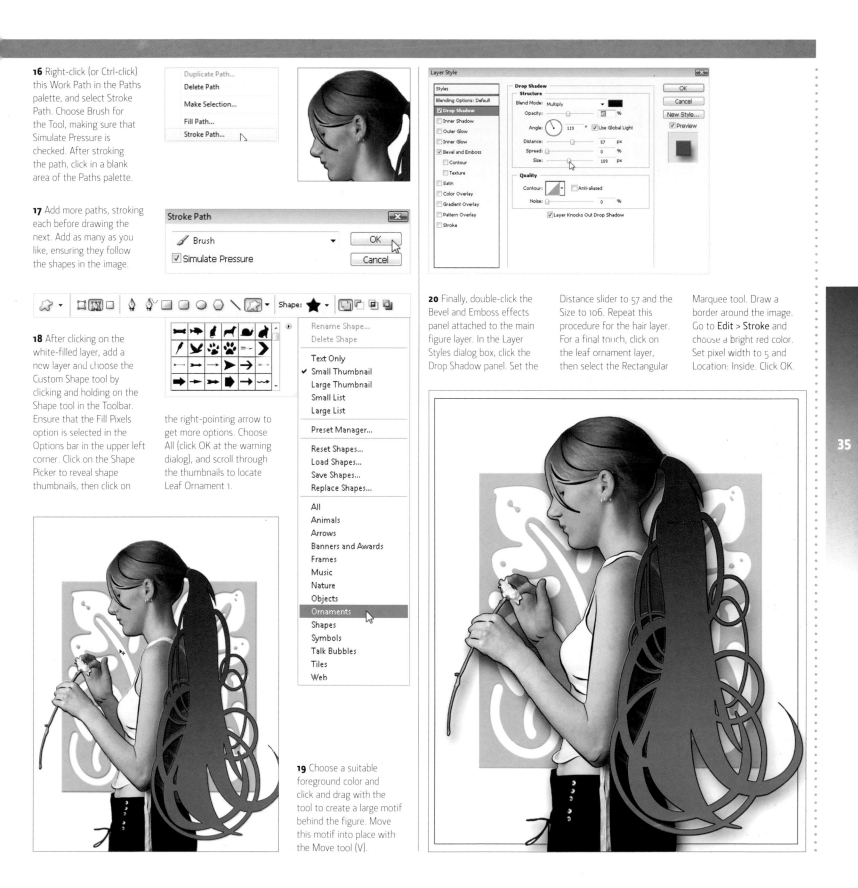

16 Right-click (or Ctrl-click) this Work Path in the Paths palette, and select Stroke Path. Choose Brush for the Tool, making sure that Simulate Pressure is checked. After stroking the path, click in a blank area of the Paths palette.

17 Add more paths, stroking each before drawing the next. Add as many as you like, ensuring they follow the shapes in the image.

18 After clicking on the white-filled layer, add a new layer and choose the Custom Shape tool by clicking and holding on the Shape tool in the Toolbar. Ensure that the Fill Pixels option is selected in the Options bar in the upper left corner. Click on the Shape Picker to reveal shape thumbnails, then click on the right-pointing arrow to get more options. Choose All (click OK at the warning dialog), and scroll through the thumbnails to locate Leaf Ornament 1.

19 Choose a suitable foreground color and click and drag with the tool to create a large motif behind the figure. Move this motif into place with the Move tool (V).

20 Finally, double-click the Bevel and Emboss effects panel attached to the main figure layer. In the Layer Styles dialog box, click the Drop Shadow panel. Set the Distance slider to 57 and the Size to 106. Repeat this procedure for the hair layer. For a final touch, click on the leaf ornament layer, then select the Rectangular Marquee tool. Draw a border around the image. Go to **Edit > Stroke** and choose a bright red color. Set pixel width to 5 and Location: Inside. Click OK.

35

Warhol screen print

Andy Warhol's silkscreen prints are recognized worldwide, and epitomize the entire Pop Art style. In this example, we'll get into the very essence of Warhol's images, most famously evident in the iconic Campbell's soup can images. But we can update the technique with our own digital twist, using Photoshop.

There are a couple of Photoshop filters that are invaluable here. The Cutout filter is a great way to simplify and break up the tones in the image, very much a characteristic of screen printing, while clever use of the Glowing Edges filter provides some solid lines for definition.

In essence, we're paying homage to a great 20th-century artist—in a 21st-century fashion.

36

1 Before we begin to simulate the screen print effect, isolate the can from its background. Select the Magic Wand tool from the Toolbar and set the Tolerance to 30 in the Options bar. Ensure that Anti-Aliased and Contiguous are both checked. Click anywhere in the white surrounding the can to generate a selection. Invert the selection using **Select > Inverse** (Ctrl/Cmd+Shift+I) so that the can itself is selected.

2 With the selection active, go to **Edit > Copy** (Ctrl/Cmd+C) and then to **Edit > Paste** (Ctrl/Cmd+V) to paste a copy of the can on a separate layer. Name this "Can layer." Duplicate this new layer by going to **Layer > Duplicate Layer** (Ctrl/Cmd+J), and name the duplicate "Glowing Edges."

3 To begin the screen-print effect, we need to establish a bold outline. With the Glowing Edges layer selected, go to **Filter > Stylize > Glowing Edges**. Use Edge Width 2, Edge Brightness 13 and Smoothness 5. Click OK.

4 Go to **Image > Adjustments > Desaturate** (Ctrl/Cmd+Shift+U) followed by **Image > Adjustments > Invert** (Ctrl/Cmd+I) so that we have a monochrome line drawing of the can. Set the blending mode for this layer to Multiply so that the original can image shows through the drawing.

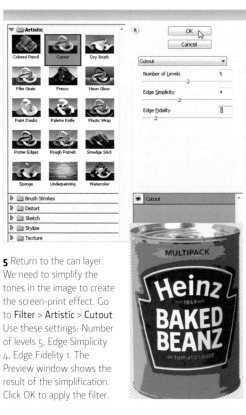

5 Return to the can layer. We need to simplify the tones in the image to create the screen-print effect. Go to **Filter > Artistic > Cutout**. Use these settings: Number of levels 5, Edge Simplicity 4, Edge Fidelity 1. The Preview window shows the result of the simplification. Click OK to apply the filter.

6 Return to the Glowing Edges layer and use the Eraser tool to erase this layer over just the small lettering on the label.

7 To create an image reminiscent of Warhol, we need to adjust the colors of the can. Return to the can layer and go to **Image > Adjustments > Hue and Saturation**. Check the Preview box, grab the Hue slider, and slide it all the way to the left. The colors in the image change as we move the slider. To increase the vibrancy of the colors, pull the Saturation slider to the right until the value reads about 75.

8 Click on the top Glowing Edges layer and go to **Layer > Merge Down** (Ctrl/Cmd+E) to merge the can and drawing layers.

9 Now, enlarge the canvas so that more images can be added. Ensure that the background color is set to white and go to **Image > Canvas Size**. In the dialog box, change the width units box to percent and enter 100 in the Width and Height boxes. Click the top left square in the Anchor plan and click OK.

10 Make three duplicate copies of the completed can layer by repeatedly dragging it to the New Layer icon in the Layers palette (or hit Ctrl/Cmd+J three times). Click on each layer in turn and use the Move tool (V) to position the four cans around the canvas. See tip box for how to align layers.

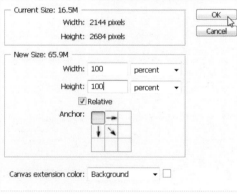

11 Now we'll alter the colors of the additional three cans. To do this, on each layer in turn go to **Image > Adjustments > Hue and Saturation** and adjust the Hue slider as in step 6, choosing a different hue for each additional can. Adjust the Saturation slider as necessary.

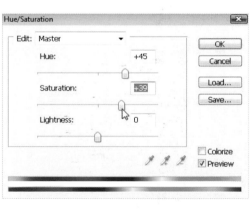

12 Finally, add a new layer at the bottom of the stack and make a selection with the Rectangular Marquee tool to cover a quarter of the total area (behind one can). Fill this selection with a color of your choice using **Edit > Fill**. Move the selection to the other quarters by dragging and filling each time with a different color.

Watercolor

Although Photoshop includes filters and effects rather optimistically labeled Watercolor, their shortcomings become all too apparent after the first few attempts to use them to produce a convincing fine art image.

In fact, the program does have the power to enable us to mimic real watercolor paintings, but success relies on good technique rather than a simple one-click process.

Although the techniques in this example are relatively basic—manipulating image layers and adding some subtle brushwork—the results are deceptively sophisticated.

A point worth noting here is that a pressure-sensitive stylus and pad is virtually essential when it comes to expressive and effective use of brushes. Using Brush Options, a brush can be set to respond directly to the pressure applied by the stylus. As a result, extremely subtle variations in the opacity and density of the brushstrokes can be achieved.

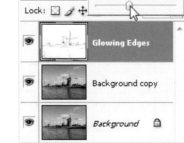

1 Duplicate the background layer (Ctrl/Cmd+J). To prepare the image for the watercolor effect, go to **Filter > Blur > Smart Blur**. This will simplify the tones and the detail in the image. Use these settings: Radius 14.1, Threshold 68.4, Quality High, Mode Normal.

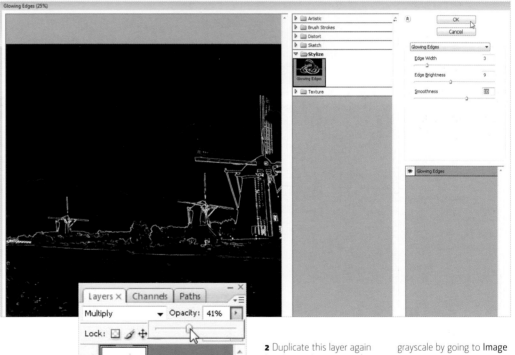

2 Duplicate this layer again (Ctrl/Cmd+J), and name it "Glowing Edges." To create the effect of an initial line drawing, go to **Filter > Stylize > Glowing Edges**. Use: Width 3, Brightness 9, and Smoothness 10. This layer needs to be inverted so there are dark lines on a light base. Go to **Image > Adjustments > Invert** (Ctrl/Cmd+I). Finally, desaturate the line work to make it grayscale by going to **Image > Adjustments > Desaturate** (Ctrl/Cmd+Shift+U). Set this layer's blending mode to Multiply, and reduce the opacity to 41%.

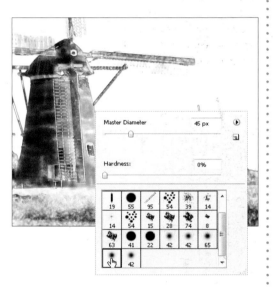

5 Hit D to ensure that the foreground color is black. Paint with this brush at a large size over the main central area of the image at an opacity of about 60%. Leave plenty of plain white around the edges of the picture. Gradually build up the depth of color by painting over certain areas more than once. To give the impression of real watercolor, it's important to leave small areas of white here and there.

3 Duplicate the first background copy layer that we applied Smart Blur to, name it "Painting Layer," and drag it to the top of the layer stack. Go to Image > Adjustments > Invert (Ctrl/Cmd+I) and set the blending mode for this layer to Color

Dodge. The image will turn white at this stage, which is exactly what we need. This will be our blank canvas. Paint onto it with black, which, because of its blending mode, will reveal the colors in the image.

6 Click in the Brush Picker again, click the right-pointing arrow, and now choose Wet Media Brushes. Select Watercolor Textured Surface from the brush thumbnails. Use the Zoom tool to zoom into the main windmill in the image. Paint with this brush (using black) into the windmill and surrounding areas. Use short, random strokes that follow the contours and shapes of the components of the image.

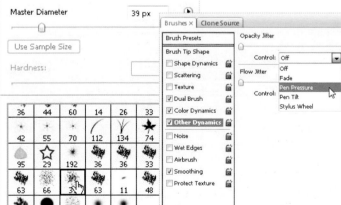

4 Select the Brush tool and click in the Brush Picker. To make sure that you are using the default brush set, click the small, right-pointing arrow and choose Reset Brushes. Next, scroll down the brush thumbnails and choose Dry Brush. If you are using a graphics tablet, hit

F5 to display the Brush Options. Click in the Other Dynamics panel, and for Opacity Jitter, choose Pressure in the Control box.

7 Use this brush to paint over the rest of the land in the image. Use short, expressive strokes. When you paint over the grass and the bushes, try to follow the direction of the grass and plant growth and use directional strokes to define the image. Gradually build up color by painting over some areas again with black at low opacity.

Watercolor continued

8 Increase the size of the brush using the right-hand square bracket, and paint large, loose strokes into the sky and water. Don't try to follow the details of the clouds or ripples in the water, just add some interest and movement with these strokes. This will give a real feeling of pure watercolor.

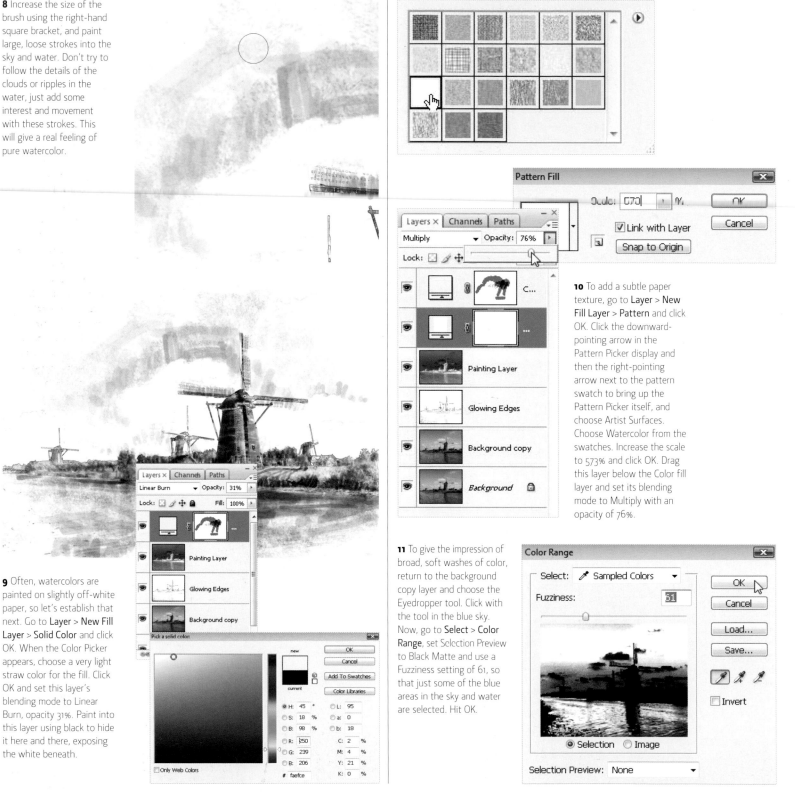

9 Often, watercolors are painted on slightly off-white paper, so let's establish that next. Go to **Layer > New Fill Layer > Solid Color** and click OK. When the Color Picker appears, choose a very light straw color for the fill. Click OK and set this layer's blending mode to Linear Burn, opacity 31%. Paint into this layer using black to hide it here and there, exposing the white beneath.

10 To add a subtle paper texture, go to **Layer > New Fill Layer > Pattern** and click OK. Click the downward-pointing arrow in the Pattern Picker display and then the right-pointing arrow next to the pattern swatch to bring up the Pattern Picker itself, and choose Artist Surfaces. Choose Watercolor from the swatches. Increase the scale to 573% and click OK. Drag this layer below the Color fill layer and set its blending mode to Multiply with an opacity of 76%.

11 To give the impression of broad, soft washes of color, return to the background copy layer and choose the Eyedropper tool. Click with the tool in the blue sky. Now, go to **Select > Color Range**, set Selection Preview to Black Matte and use a Fuzziness setting of 61, so that just some of the blue areas in the sky and water are selected. Hit OK.

40

12 Go to **Edit > Copy** (Ctrl/Cmd+C), **Edit > Paste** (Ctrl/Cmd+V). Drag this newly pasted blue layer up so that it sits directly below the Pattern Fill layer. Go to **Filter > Blur > Motion Blur**. Use these settings: Angle 90, Distance 283. Set this layer to Darken blending mode, opacity 60%.

13 To complete the image, duplicate the background copy layer again, name it "Watercolor Filter," and drag this copy to the top of the layer stack. We'll emphasize the overall effect by using Photoshop's Watercolor filter very subtly. Go to **Filter > Artistic > Watercolor**. Use: Brush Detail 12, Shadow Intensity 0, Texture 3. Click OK to apply the filter. Finally, set this layer's blending mode to Luminosity, and the opacity to 27% so that it just adds a touch of emphasis to the painting.

14 Return to the Painting layer and choose the Brush tool. Click in the Brush Picker, selecting the Watercolor Heavy Loaded brush. Hit D on the keyboard to revert to default colors. Using black, paint some small strokes throughout the center of interest in the image. This brush produces distinct, sharp accents that will help to direct the viewer's attention.

Tip

MAKING MARKS
Although this technique results in a convincing painterly effect, you really don't need to be an accomplished artist to successfully create it. All we're actually doing here is making simple marks with the brush, using black on the Color Dodge layer. Due to the blending mode of this layer, the black marks allow the colors on the underlying layer to show through at various opacities. Because of the special qualities of the brushes used, the black marks on the layer have the effect and texture of real watercolor on paper. It's important to ensure that the marks we make on this layer are energetic and lively. As a general rule, short dabs work better than long strokes.

Oil painting

There are many filters out there that promise to transform digital photographs into oil paintings, but it has to be said that most fail miserably. To create a truly realistic oil painting effect we need to be a little more inventive. One of the most important characteristics of an oil painting is the contrast of thin areas of paint set against areas of thick, solid paint or impasto. Another vitally important factor is texture. Oil paintings have a surface quality that is unique to the medium itself, and for the effect to
be convincing we need to mimic this accurately. Fortunately, Photoshop has a selection of brushes that are made for this very purpose. These brushes can apply color and convincing textures at the same time. For the thick impasto effect, we can employ a layer style that will give the brushstroke a subtle 3D quality.

Remember, this project will be far more successful if a pressure-sensitive graphics tablet is used, as the brushes we're going to use have properties that respond directly to stylus pressure.

1 To begin the painting, make a toned canvas layer for the final image to be "painted" onto. With the start image open, add a new layer (Ctrl/Cmd+Shift+N), naming the layer "Canvas." Choose a warm gray for the foreground color and go to **Edit > Fill > Use Foreground color**. We'll add a canvas texture to this background a little later.

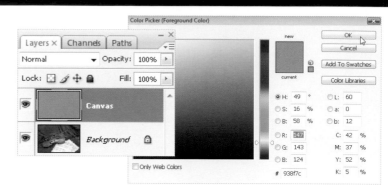

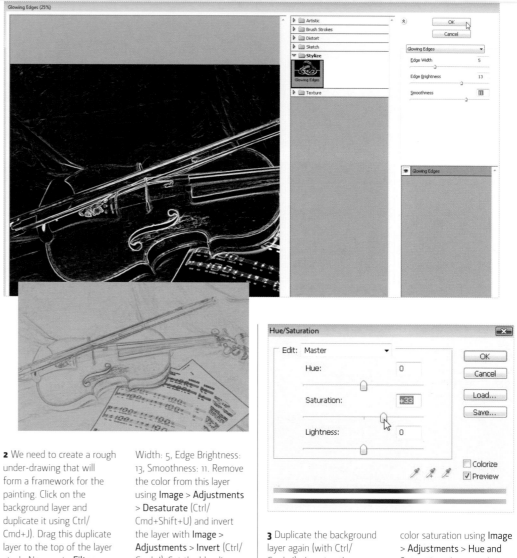

2 We need to create a rough under-drawing that will form a framework for the painting. Click on the background layer and duplicate it using Ctrl/Cmd+J. Drag this duplicate layer to the top of the layer stack. Now go to **Filter > Stylize > Glowing Edges**. Use these settings: Edge Width: 5, Edge Brightness: 13, Smoothness: 11. Remove the color from this layer using **Image > Adjustments > Desaturate** (Ctrl/Cmd+Shift+U) and invert the layer with **Image > Adjustments > Invert** (Ctrl/Cmd+I). Set the blending mode for this layer to Multiply, opacity to 57%.

3 Duplicate the background layer again (with Ctrl/Cmd+J), dragging the duplicate to the top of the layer stack. Increase the color saturation using **Image > Adjustments > Hue and Saturation**, dragging the Saturation slider up to 33.

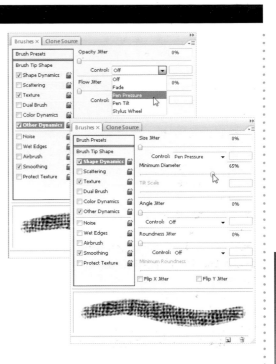

6 Hit F5 to display the Brush Options. Click the Texture category and increase the Texture Scale to 85%. Choose Shape Dynamics, setting the Minimum Diameter to 65%. Finally, if using a graphics tablet, choose Other Dynamics and set Opacity Jitter Control to Pen Pressure.

4 To lose some of the detail in the image and begin to create a painterly effect, go to **Filter** > **Artistic** > **Palette Knife**. Use 12 for Stroke Size, 2 for Stroke Detail, and 10 for Softness. Click OK to apply the filter. Set the blending mode for this layer to Hard Light.

5 Hide this layer with a mask, using **Layer** > **Layer Mask** > **Hide All**. We need to set up the properties of a particular brush, so choose the Brush tool and click in the Brush Picker. Hit the right-pointing arrow in the Picker, select Wet Media Brushes, and choose Brush Light Texture Medium Tip from the brush thumbnails.

7 Select white as the foreground color. Working on the layer mask, begin to paint over the image. Make sure to leave some gaps here and there, allowing the canvas to show through the painted areas. Use the brush at varying sizes to introduce some interest.

8 In a traditional oil painting, the dark areas are painted thinly and the light areas are painted with thick paint, or impasto, so bear this in mind as you continue to paint into the image, overlaying more brushstrokes in the light areas.

Oil painting continued

9 As you paint, you'll see that because we've chosen a brush that carries texture with its stroke, you begin to create a convincing "paint on canvas" effect with the brushstrokes. At this stage, don't worry about painting over the fabric that the objects are lying on, just concentrate on the violin and sheet music.

10 As you get toward the outside edges of the painting, make your brushstrokes far less opaque and more sketchy. Control the opacity of the Brush either using the slider in the Options bar or, if you're using a graphics tablet, by the pressure applied to the stylus.

11 Now duplicate this main Painting layer, complete with Layer Mask, by going to **Layer > Duplicate Layer**. To give the impression of thick paint on the layer, add a Layer Style. Go to **Layer >**

Layer Style > Bevel and Emboss. For Style choose Emboss, and increase the Depth slide to 81.

12 Click on the layer mask for this layer in the Layers palette and fill it with black using **Edit > Fill > Use: Black**. This will completely hide the image layer, ready for some more painting.

13 Return to the Brush tool and continue to paint with white. Remember to make sure that you are painting on the Layer Mask and not the actual image layer by checking for a bold outline around the thumbnail for the mask in the Layers palette. Concentrate on painting mainly into the lighter areas in the image with the brush at a fairly small size. As you paint, you'll see the effect of thick paint standing on the surface of the canvas begin to develop.

14 Change brushes to add a few more deft strokes of impasto that will really add to the oil painting effect. Click in the Brush Picker and choose Oil Medium To Large Tip. In Brush Options, select Shape Dynamics and set Opacity Jitter Control to Pen Pressure. Next, choose Shape Dynamics and set Minimum Diameter to 75%. Again, painting with white, add a few stokes here and there with this brush.

44

15 Now, right-click/Ctrl-click each layer mask in turn, choosing Apply Layer Mask on both. This will apply the mask to the image layer, maintaining the transparency values from the masks. Click on the topmost painting layer and go to **Layer > Merge Down** (Ctrl/Cmd+E) to merge the two painting layers together.

16 Select the Smudge tool from the Toolbar. Choose the Oil Medium To Large Tip brush again from the Brush Picker. Bring up the Brush Options; in Shape Dynamics set Minimum Diameter to 75%. If using a graphics tablet, go to the Other Dynamics category and set

Strength Jitter to Pen Pressure. Now, using this tool on the Palette Knife layer, gently smudge parts of the image, paying special attention to smudging edges here and there. This will give the impression of some nice loose brushwork.

Tip

PRINTING PERFECTION! To add the perfect finishing touch to our "oil painting," try printing the finished image onto canvas-textured media. There are many manufacturers out there that produce canvas-type inkjet papers, and some real artists' canvas can be used in a normal inkjet printer. The advantage to using this is that the subtle canvas textures we've added using Photoshop's special brushes are enhanced by the physical surface texture of the canvas.

It's worth making a test print first, to see if printing on the canvas paper produces any unwanted color shifts. Compensate for this by adjusting the Hue/Saturation in Photoshop before making the final print (it may take a few test prints to get it just right). Remember to always follow the manufacturer's instructions regarding media-type settings for your printer.

45

17 To complete the painting, we need to apply a canvas texture to the Canvas layer. Click on the Canvas layer in the Layers palette and go to **Filter > Texture > Texturizer**. In the Texturizer dialog box, choose Canvas for Texture, 176% for Scaling, 10 for Relief, and Top Left for Light Direction. Click OK to apply the texture. To finish, flatten the image with **Layer > Flatten Image** and save.

Pencil sketch

Ask any artist and they'll tell you that all the tubes of paint in the world cannot replace the simple pencil when it comes to artistic potential. Through the centuries, the litmus test of an artist's ability was demonstrated best through the medium of drawing. In days of yore, student painters spent years drawing with graphite to hone their skills. The so-called "Sketch Filters" in Photoshop consistently yield very disappointing results, so re-creating the quintessential sketch demands a little more inventiveness and an approach that mimics traditional techniques.

Pencil sketches work especially well when very soft-leaded pencils are used on a tinted paper, with a few touches of white chalk here and there to heighten the tones. This is what we'll produce here, digitally. Don't worry if your drawing abilities aren't up to snuff, all that's required here is the ability to scribble!

1 Open the start image in Photoshop. Go to **Layer > New Fill Layer > Solid Color**, call it "Gray Fill," and click OK. In the Color Picker, choose a light gray.

2 Click the "Create new fill or adjustment layer" icon at the base of the Layers palette and choose Pattern from the list. Click in the Pattern Swatch in the dialog box, hit the right-pointing arrow, and select Grayscale Paper. Choose Fibers 1 from the swatch. Increase the Pattern Scale to 340% and click OK. Set this layer to Soft Light, and 35% opacity.

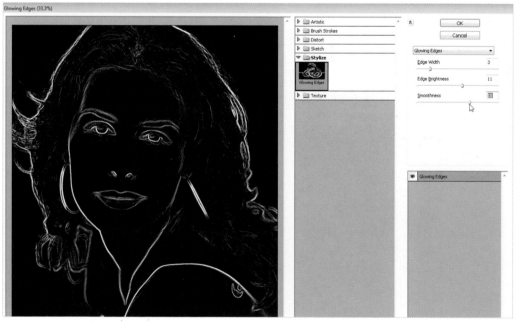

3 Right-click/Ctrl-click the background layer and choose Duplicate Layer, calling the layer "Glowing Edges." Drag this new layer to the top of the stack and go to **Filter > Stylize > Glowing Edges**. Use these values: Edge Width 3, Edge Brightness 11, Smoothness 10.

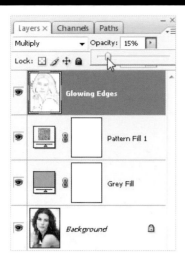

4 Invert the Glowing Edges layer, using **Image > Adjustments > Invert** (Ctrl/Cmd+I). This layer only needs to be black and white, so go to **Image > Adjustments > Desaturate** (Ctrl/Cmd+Shift+U). Set the layer's blending mode to Multiply with an opacity of 15%.

6 We need to add some Noise to this layer to break the image up a little, so go to **Filter > Noise > Add Noise**. Use an Amount of 12%, choose Gaussian for Distribution, and check Monochromatic.

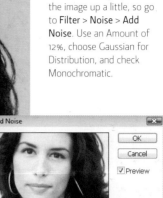

5 Duplicate the background layer again, calling it "Sketch Layer," and drag this duplicate to the top of the stack. Desaturate this layer using **Image > Adjustments > Desaturate** (Ctrl/Cmd+Shift+U). To use the layer as a base for the drawing, increase the contrast a little, by going to **Image > Adjustments > Brightness and Contrast**. Drag the Contrast slider to the right to a value of 22. Now, set the layer blending mode to Darken and leave the opacity set to 100%.

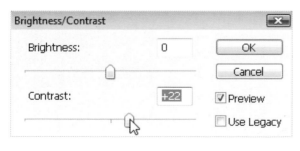

7 Add a Hide All layer mask to this layer, using **Layer > Layer Mask > Hide All**. To make the drawing, simply scribble on this layer mask using a special brush.

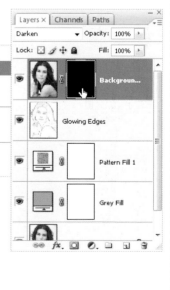

Pencil sketch continued

8 Select the Brush tool and click in the Brush Picker. Click the right-pointing arrow in the Picker and choose Dry Media Brushes. Scroll down the thumbnails and double-click Pastel on Charcoal Paper.

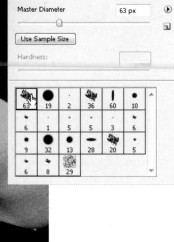

10 Be sure that the foreground color swatch is white. In the Options bar, increase the size of the brush to between 20 and 25 pixels. Now, begin to scribble onto the Sketch Layer's layer mask. At first, just concentrate on the main facial features within the image. Use just a little pressure on the stylus, or a very low opacity for the brush. Scribble loosely over all of the required parts of the image, changing direction often to create a hand-shaded look.

48

9 If you're using a graphics tablet, hit F5 on the keyboard to display the Brush Options. Click the Other Dynamics panel and set the Opacity Jitter Control box to Pen Pressure. Click Shape Dynamics and set the Size Jitter to Pen Pressure. Set Minimum Diameter to 70%. Remember, if you are not using a graphics tablet, you must control the opacity of the Brush using the Opacity slider in the Options bar.

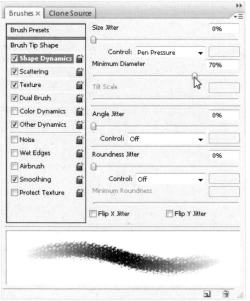

11 Use plenty of cross-hatch scribble where the strokes overlap in opposite directions. Remember, there is no actual drawing ability whatsoever required here, we are simply scribbling to reveal the layer lying beneath the Layer mask.

12 Increase the size of the brush a little by using the right-facing square bracket key on the keyboard. Continue to scribble over the image, remembering to keep the brushwork nice and loose, building up the tones around the features of the face. In the hair, and around the outside of the image, use the brush at a bigger size and make the strokes even more sketchy.

13 Finally, reduce the size of the brush again and use it with white at full opacity to scribble more into the main features, adding some really dark strokes.

49

Pen-and-ink drawing

Pen-and-ink drawings have a charm all of their own. There is a certain crispness and clarity to a pen drawing that can't be achieved in any other way. As a technique, it's quite a challenge to replicate in Photoshop, although by no means impossible. Pen drawings rely on the density of hatched lines to create varying tones within an image, and, where the individual lines are black in color, the viewer's eye interprets different densities of hatching as various shades of gray.

Pen drawings evoke an antique "old world" feeling. The technique seems especially suited to architectural subjects.

To create the pen-and-ink effect, we'll use Photoshop's Graphic Pen filter. This filter has to be used with care, as it's a stock effect, which, when used on a single layer does not produce a satisfactory result. However, combining a number of layers with different settings will replicate the technique employed by artists, who use pen strokes at different angles.

1 To use the Graphic Pen filter effectively, the background color must be set to white, so be sure that this is done before we start (hit D on the keyboard or click on the black and white color swatches near the bottom of the Toolbar).

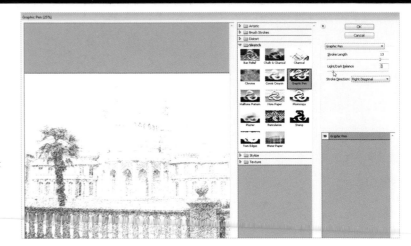

2 Start by making four copies of the background layer (hit Ctrl/Cmd+J four times). Click on the topmost duplicate layer and rename it "Pen layer." Then go to **Filter > Sketch > Graphic Pen**, and enter these settings: Stroke Length: 13, Light/Dark Balance: 8, and select Right Diagonal for Direction.

Tip

PAPER TEXTURE

To add a little extra realism to the Pen Drawing, try adding a subtle paper texture to the finished image. After the drawing is completed, go to Layer > New Fill Layer > Pattern. Click in the small pattern swatch and load Artist Surfaces using the small right pointing arrow. Choose a texture from the swatches and increase the Scale to at least 300%. Set this pattern layer

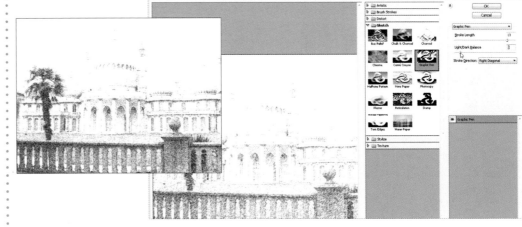

3 To sharpen the pen strokes on this layer, apply **Filter > Sharpen > Sharpen Edges** twice. Then drag one of the remaining background copies to the top of the layer stack

and rename it "Darken 1." Go to **Filter > Sketch > Graphic Pen**, but this time use: Stroke Length: 9, Light/Dark Balance: 8, and choose Left Diagonal for

Direction. Set the layer blending mode to Darken, allowing the underlying layer to show through.

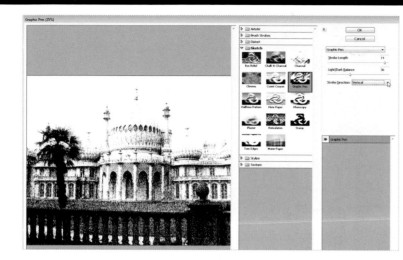

4 Drag another of the background copies to the top of the stack and name it "Darken 2." Click on the layer, then go to **Image > Adjustments > Brightness and Contrast**. To create a more subtle effect, reduce the contrast by pulling the Contrast slider to the left, setting it at -20. Go to **Filter > Sketch > Graphic Pen**, and apply: Stroke Length: 14, Light/Dark Balance: 36, and Direction: Vertical. Set the blending mode to Darken, with an opacity of 75%.

6 The pen-and-ink drawing is complete at this stage, but we might want to add some subtle watercolor wash effects to the image. To do this, duplicate the background layer, and drag it to the top of the layer stack. Go to **Filter > Blur > Gaussian Blur**, with a radius of 30. Set the layer blend mode to Color.

51

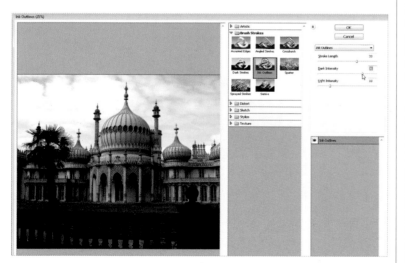

5 Add some loosely drawn outlines by dragging the remaining background copy to the top of the stack. Rename it "Ink layer." Go to **Filter > Brush Strokes > Ink Outlines**, and apply these settings: Stroke Length: 33, Dark Intensity: 38, and Light Intensity: 10. To remove color from this layer, desaturate it using **Image > Adjustments > Desaturate** (Ctrl/Cmd+ Shift+U). Set the layer blending mode to Hard Light, with opacity of 54%.

Woodcut and linocut

Making prints from a woodcut—a printing block created by gouging a design into a wooden block—is a technique that dates back to the earliest days of printing.

Essentially, the design on the block is carved into the wood in reverse. When the block is inked with a flat roller, the areas that have been carved don't pick up any ink, while the areas that haven't been carved do. When printed, only the uncarved areas leave an impression. There are a few Photoshop techniques that can be found on the Internet for simulating this printing technique, but here we'll use one that involves using vector paths, which produce the sharp lines and fills ideally suited to this effect.

So, digital wood chisels at the ready, we're about to create a woodcut print...

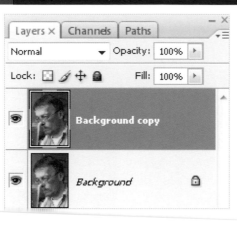

1 To create the woodcut effect, we need first to dramatically simplify the start images in various stages. Begin by copying the background layer (Ctrl/Cmd+J).

2 On this duplicate layer, go to **Image** > **Adjustments** > **Threshold**. Drag the pointer to the left to a Threshold value of 75 and click OK. It's immediately apparent how much this simplifies the image tones.

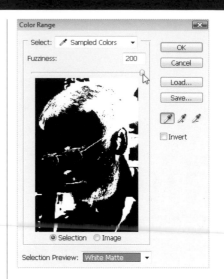

3 Now hit D on the keyboard to revert to the default black/white swatch colors. Go to **Select** > **Color Range** and drag the Fuzziness slider up to a maximum of 200. This will select just the blacks in the image.

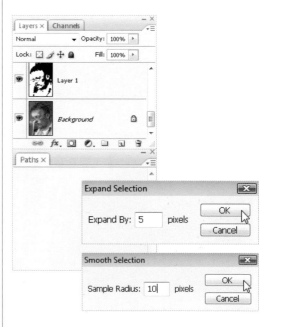

4 Go to **Select** > **Modify** > **Expand**, using a value of 5 pixels. Then, simplify with **Select** > **Modify** > **Smooth**. For Sample Radius, enter 10 pixels. Now, click on the Paths palette and drag this palette out into the workspace.

5 At the base of the Paths palette, click on the "Make work path from selection" icon. Wait while Photoshop converts the Selection into a Path. Now go to **Edit** > **Fill**, choosing White for Contents to fill the duplicate layer with white, leaving just the Path visible.

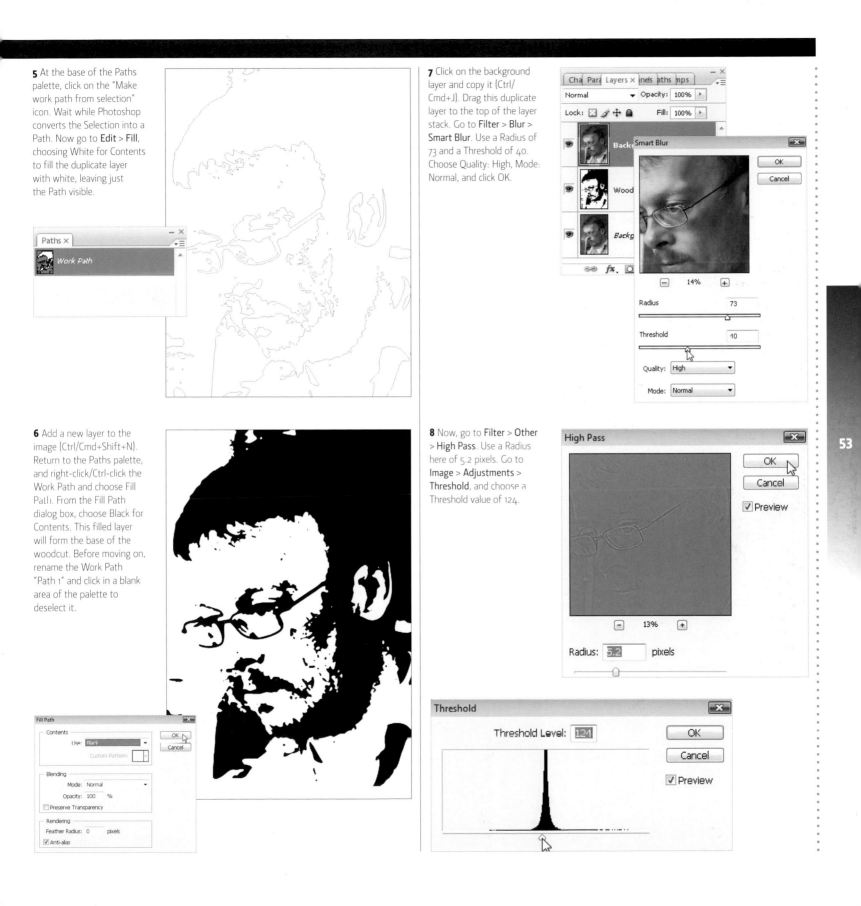

6 Add a new layer to the image (Ctrl/Cmd+Shift+N). Return to the Paths palette, and right-click/Ctrl-click the Work Path and choose Fill Path. From the Fill Path dialog box, choose Black for Contents. This filled layer will form the base of the woodcut. Before moving on, rename the Work Path "Path 1" and click in a blank area of the palette to deselect it.

7 Click on the background layer and copy it (Ctrl/Cmd+J). Drag this duplicate layer to the top of the layer stack. Go to **Filter** > **Blur** > **Smart Blur**. Use a Radius of 73 and a Threshold of 40. Choose Quality: High, Mode: Normal, and click OK.

8 Now, go to **Filter** > **Other** > **High Pass**. Use a Radius here of 5.2 pixels. Go to **Image** > **Adjustments** > **Threshold**, and choose a Threshold value of 124.

Woodcut and linocut continued

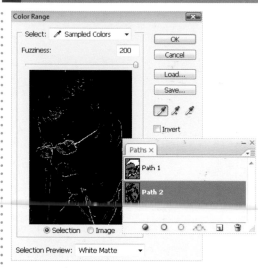

9 Select **Image > Adjustments > Invert** (Ctrl/ Cmd+I), and then hit X on the keyboard to swap the foreground and background colors so white is foreground. Go to **Select > Color Range**, again using a Fuzziness of 200. Now, again go to **Select > Modify > Smooth**, using a Sample Radius of 5 pixels. Return to the Paths palette, choose the "Make work path from selection" icon again, and name this "Path 2." Grab this duplicate layer in the Layers palette and drag it to the trash can.

11 Duplicate the background layer for a final time, dragging it to the top of the stack. We need to use a different technique here to add a little detail to the image. Go to **Filter > Stylize > Glowing Edges**. Use: Edge Width 6, Edge Brightness 11, Smoothness 14.

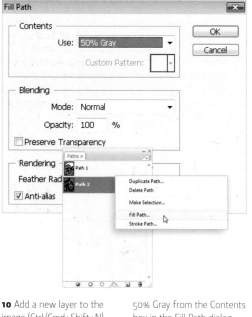

10 Add a new layer to the image (Ctrl/Cmd+Shift+N). Now, right-click/Ctrl-click Path 2 in the Paths palette and choose Fill Path. Choose 50% Gray from the Contents box in the Fill Path dialog box. This will add a little detail to the woodcut image. Click off the Work Path.

12 Return to **Image > Adjustments > Threshold**, choosing a Threshold level of 107. Be sure that the foreground color is white. Then, go to **Select > Color Range**, again using a maximum Fuzziness value of 200. Go to **Select > Modify > Smooth** and set a Sample Radius of 5.

54

Tip

WOODCUT PRINT ON COLORED GROUND

It's easy to recreate the effect of the final woodcut printed on a colored paper. When the image is completed, with the layers still intact, click on the Woodcut 1 layer and go to Layer > New Fill Layer > Solid Color. Choose a color for the ground from the picker, and then simply set the blending mode for the Color Fill layer to Linear Burn in the Layers palette.

If you want to print the image directly onto colored paper, then you will first need to delete the background layer (convert it into a normal layer first by double-clicking it). Depending on the color of the paper that you're printing onto, you may also want to delete the colored layer, leaving just the black and
gray layers.

13 Again, convert the selection to a Work Path in the Paths palette. Drag the duplicate layer to the trash can and add a final new layer (Ctrl/Cmd+ Shift+N). Click the foreground color swatch choosing a light orange/ tan from the Color Picker. Right-click/Ctrl-click the Work Path in the Paths palette, choosing Fill Path. From the Fill Path dialog box, choose foreground color for Contents. Click off the Work Path and drag this layer below the gray-filled woodcut layer. Finally, use the Eraser tool to erase any unwanted parts from each layer.

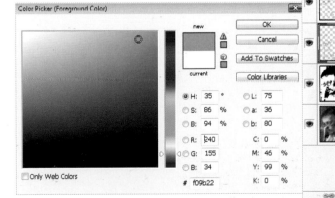

LIGHTING EFFECTS

Adding rays of light

Light is the essence of photography—and it's also the photographer's most effective tool for creating unique images, with power and romance that set them apart from ordinary snapshots. Unfortunately, time and nature are not always on our side when it comes to this most alchemic photographic ingredient. But all is not lost. Armed with Photoshop, we can add stunning lighting effects, even after the fact. To simulate the subtle and mysterious qualities of light, gradients and layer masks are our greatest allies.

In this example, we'll use gradients to recreate the effect of light passing through a stained-glass window. Using different gradients on separate layers with various blending mode settings, we can simulate the effect of dissipating light beams with great authenticity. By making selections for each beam of light with the Polygon Lasso tool, we can accurately restrict the gradient fills and then lightly blur the edges. We can then adjust the direction of each light beam layer by using Transform. Photographs need never be hampered by dull, gray days again.

1 Begin by adding an overall shaft of light that will serve as the foundation for the final lighting effect. Add a new layer (Ctrl/Cmd+ Shift+N), call it "Main Beam," and then select the Pen tool. Draw a large wedge-shaped path from the very top of the window, radiating out over to the left side of the image.

2 The path should encompass the entire bottom left-hand corner of the image. Click again with the tool at each corner of the shape. Click at the bottom right of the window, and again where the top curve begins. Now, return to the starting point, clicking and dragging to follow the curve.

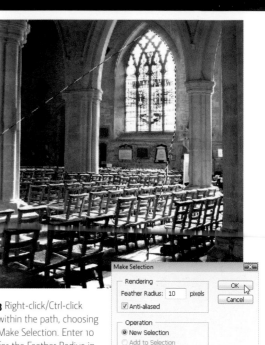

3 Right-click/Ctrl-click within the path, choosing Make Selection. Enter 10 for the Feather Radius in the dialog box and hit OK.

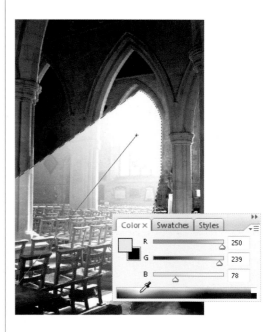

4 Choose a very pale yellow from the Color palette (accessed under Window, if it's not already open) and choose the Gradient tool. Click in the Gradient Picker and choose Foreground to Transparent. Select Linear Gradient in the Options bar, and drag a gradient from the top of the window to the bottom left-hand corner. Hit Ctrl/ Cmd+D to deselect.

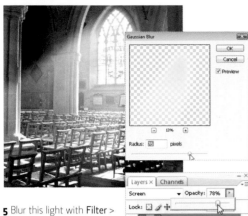

5 Blur this light with **Filter > Blur > Gaussian Blur**, using a Blur Radius of 76 pixels. Set the layer blending mode to Screen and reduce the layer opacity to 78%.

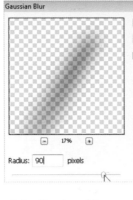

7 Soften the edges of the beam with a Gaussian Blur at a radius setting of 90 pixels (**Filter > Blur > Gaussian Blur**). Change the blending mode for this layer to Vivid Light, and reduce the opacity to create a subtle, convincing effect.

9 To give the effect of the light being filtered by airborne particles, return to the Main Beam layer and go to **Filter > Noise > Add Noise**. Select Gaussian for Distribution and use an Amount of 20%.

10 We can adjust the exact hue of each light beam by clicking on it in the Layers palette and going to **Image > Adjustments > Hue/ Saturation**. Use the Hue slider to modify the color and increase or decrease the brightness using the Lightness slider.

59

6 To heighten the effect, we now need to add some colored light beams. Create a new layer called "Colored Beams." Choose the Polygon Lasso tool and draw a thin light beam, radiating from the main red glass in the window. Ensure that the direction matches the previous beam. Choose a vivid pink and click the Gradient tool again. Drag the gradient over the length of the selection.

8 Add two thinner light rays with the Polygon Lasso on a separate layer. Fill these with a Blue-to-Transparent gradient, and blur by the same method. Set this layer to Multiply and reduce the opacity.

Tip

POLYGON LASSO: FINISH AT THE START!

Remember, when using the Polygon Lasso tool to make a selection, you need to close the selection by returning to your starting point. As you return to the point where you made your first click with the tool, a tiny circle will appear by the side of the mouse pointer, indicating that you're about to complete the selection.

Simulating studio lighting

High-quality studio shots can be tricky to pull off when all that's available is a studio the size of a broom closet. However, with a little skill and imagination, it's possible to build a virtual studio around a model—and even add realistic studio lighting—with Photoshop. The key to this technique is the powerful Lighting Effects filter. Just follow these steps and the restrictive walls of that studio will soon fall away!

60

Lighting Effects dialog box

Style: Default
Save... Delete
OK Cancel

Light type: Spotlight
☑ On
Intensity: Negative — 35 — Full
Focus: Narrow — 69 — Wide

Properties:
Gloss: Matte — 0 — Shiny
Material: Plastic — 69 — Metallic
Exposure: Under — 0 — Over
Ambience: Negative — 8 — Positive

Texture Channel: None
☑ White is high
Height: Flat — 50 — Mountainous

☑ Preview

LIGHTING EFFECTS FILTER:
The majority of adjustments within the Lighting Effects filter dialog box take place within the preview window. First, make sure that the Preview box is checked, so you can gauge the results as you make adjustments. The circle with the handles around it defines the pool of light, with the highest concentration of light along the axis line bisecting the pool. The light can be moved by clicking and dragging the central spot in the light. Pull on the outer handles of the light to widen the pool of light, and use the handles aligned with the axis to control the range of the light. The Light Type and Properties sliders control the intensity of the light and the effect it has on the subject.

Tip

EDIT > TRANSFORM
Distort transformations can be difficult at first. Try to identify which handles around the box need to be moved to achieve the desired shape, and if you're not happy, hit the stop sign next to the checkmark in the Options bar and

1 Open the main backdrop image, which we'll be using as a close-up. Using the Crop tool, crop from the top of the image to just below the lower lip.

2 To add the texture to the image, open the Channels palette and click the "Create new channel" icon at the base of the palette. Reset the color swatch to default (D). Now, go to **Filter > Render > Clouds**. This channel will be used for the lighting texture.

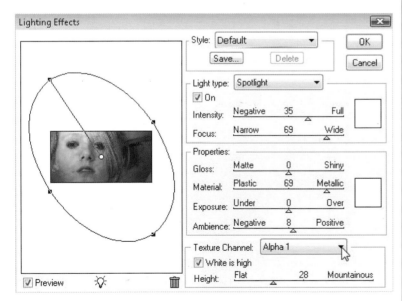

3 In the Channels palette, click back on the RGB channel before returning to the Layers tab. Now, go to **Filter > Render > Lighting Effects**. Spread the light in the preview box over the entire image, and set the height slider to 28. From the texture channel box, choose Alpha 1 as the channel to be used.

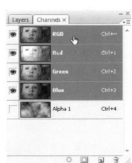

4 Go to **Image > Canvas Size** and increase the canvas size by 30% downward (click the top center in the Anchor box). At the bottom of the Toolbar, choose a deep red for the background color and a lighter shade for the foreground by clicking the respective swatches.

5 Add a new layer (Ctrl/Cmd+Shift+N), call it "Floor," and select the Rectangular Marquee tool. Drag a selection over the entire white portion at the bottom of the image. Click on the Gradient tool, choose Foreground to Background from the Gradient Picker, and drag the tool over the selection from left to right.

6 Add some Noise to this layer (**Filter > Noise > Add Noise**). Check the Monochromatic box and use a value of 13%. Press Ctrl/Cmd+D to deselect.

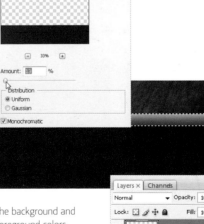

7 To add the wooden bar at the base of the backdrop, add another new layer (Ctrl/Cmd+Shift+N) and call it "Bar." With the Rectangular Marquee tool, drag a long thin selection along the base of the backdrop, across the entire width of the image. Choose light brown and dark brown for the background and foreground colors respectively, and click on the Gradient tool. Drag a gradient vertically across the selection. Finally, add some noise (**Filter > Noise > Add Noise**) and choose **Filter > Blur > Blur More**.

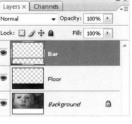

Simulating studio lighting continued

8 Add another new layer for the ropes. Choose the Pen tool from the Toolbar and click the start point at the top of the image. To create subtle curves in the path, click and pull the Pen tool slightly on the subsequent points. Choose an off-white color for the foreground and click the Paths palette tab.

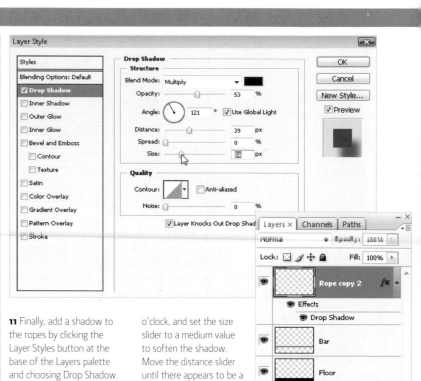

9 Select the Brush tool and choose a small, hard brush. Right-click/Ctrl-click New Work Path in the Paths palette and choose Stroke Path, selecting Brush as the tool, and ensuring that Simulate Pressure is checked. Click OK. Click away from the Work Path before returning to the Layers palette.

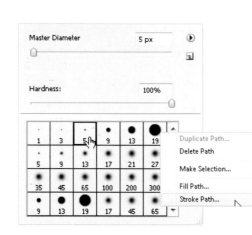

11 Finally, add a shadow to the ropes by clicking the Layer Styles button at the base of the Layers palette and choosing Drop Shadow. In the Drop Shadow dialog box, place the cross in the light direction indicator at 11 o'clock, and set the size slider to a medium value to soften the shadow. Move the distance slider until there appears to be a little distance between the ropes and the backdrop.

10 Go to **Filter > Blur > Blur More** and duplicate the Rope layer twice (Ctrl/Cmd+J). Move these new layers into position at intervals further along the backdrop. On the middle Rope layer, go to **Edit > Transform > Flip Horizontal**. Now, select these three layers and go to **Layer > Merge Layers**. Click on the Brush tool and join these ropes with a loose line. Add a couple of knots where the ropes join this line.

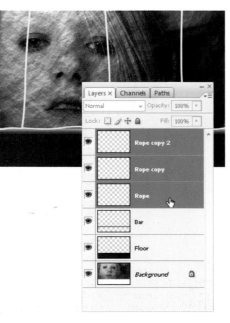

12 To add the figure, open the image of the sitting girl. Click on the Move tool, and drag this image into the main composition. Use the bounding box corners to resize the image if necessary; remember to hold down the Shift key to retain the correct proportions.

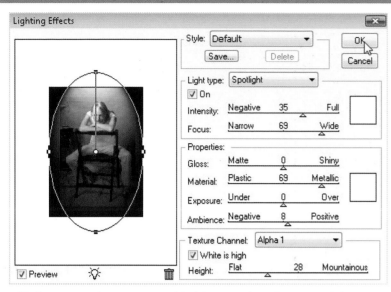

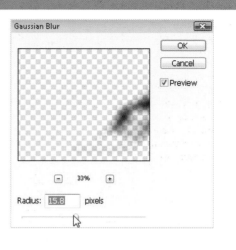

13 The figure now needs to be lit to blend into the surrounding environment. Go to **Filter** > **Render** > **Lighting Effects**. Using the default spotlight, drag the main center of the light to sit mid-body on the figure. Refer to the screenshot and expand the light circle so that it envelops the entire upper half of the figure.

Experiment with the various sliders to achieve the effect of light concentrated on the upper half of the body.

16 Set the layer blending mode for this layer to Multiply, lower the opacity, and drag the layer in the Layers palette so that it sits below the layer containing the sitting figure. Add some blur to the Shadow layer by going to **Filter** > **Blur** > **Gaussian Blur**. Finally, duplicate this layer (Ctrl/Cmd+J), go to **Edit** > **Transform** > **Distort**, and skew the new layer in the other direction. Again, make sure this layer sits below the main figure in the layer stack.

17 To add the picture on the floor, open the image and drag it into the main composition. Go to **Edit** > **Transform** > **Distort** and skew the image as before. Adjust the corner handles to achieve the desired effect.

14 Using the Lasso tool or Quick Mask, select the girl on the chair and remove the background behind her. To make the shadows, copy the sitting figure layer. Ctrl/Cmd-click the duplicate sitting figure layer thumbnail to make a selection from its transparency. Fill this selection with black; **Edit** > **Fill** > **Use: Black**. This Shadow layer now needs to be transformed so that it is cast away from, and behind, the figure. Hit Ctrl/Cmd+D to deselect.

15 On this Shadow layer, go to **Edit** > **Transform** > **Distort**. The distort box has handles around it which can be dragged to distort the layer. Click and drag on the top center handle and drag it to the right to skew the shadow. Adjust the corner handles to create the effect of perspective. Ensure that the shadow of the chair lines up with the actual chair legs on the image layer. Hit the Commit checkmark.

18 Move the image into place and go to **Filter** > **Render** > **Lighting Effects**. Position the light so that it illuminates only half of the image. Finally, click the Layer Styles button at the base of the Layers palette and apply a drop shadow to this layer.

63

Creating a neon sign

O f all forms of lighting and illumination, neon is arguably the most evocative. The result of applying an electrical charge to a tube filled with the inert gas, neon, is a light that glows with vibrancy and color. The effect of these lights, synonymous with night clubs, late-night cafés, and the famous gambling strips of Las Vegas, is relatively easy to recreate in Photoshop.

Many tutorials tell us that this can be done using the Glow family of Layer Styles, and while this is true to some extent, the effects produced with those techniques tend to lack subtlety. Here, we're going to use a less automated method, but one that produces far more realistic results.

The key to the technique is the Type tool. With this tool, we can establish the framework for the individual letters and generate pixel-accurate selections that can then be stroked with color. The Gaussian Blur filter is called into service to supply the glow around the tubes of light, and we'll also tailor the perspective of the newly created sign with the Transform function to seamlessly fit it into the image.

Once the essentials of the technique have been mastered, the potential for creating custom neon elements to add to digital photographs is almost limitless.

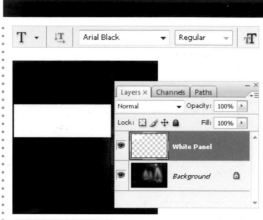

1 Open the nighttime street image and add a new layer (Ctrl/Cmd+Shift+N). Select the Rectangular Marquee tool and drag a rectangle roughly the same size as the empty space above the doorway. Now, fill this selection with white using **Edit** > **Fill** > **Use: White**. Hit Ctrl/Cmd+D to deselect.

2 Select the Horizontal Type tool and choose Arial Black from the Font Picker. Click in the white rectangle and type "CELLAR BAR." Highlight the words, and then, in the Options bar, increase the size of the type to fit the height of the white panel. Hit the Commit checkmark.

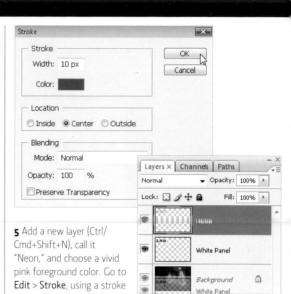

3 Right-click/Ctrl-click the Type layer (not the thumbnail) in the Layers palette, and choose Rasterize Type. Now go to **Edit** > **Transform** > **Scale** and use the handles at each end of the bounding box to fit the words to the white panel. Again, hit the checkmark in the Options bar when this is done.

4 Go to **Layer** > **Merge Down**. We need to blur the lettering slightly to achieve rounded corners, so go to **Filter** > **Blur** > **Gaussian Blur**, using a Radius of 5.2 pixels. Choose the Magic Wand and select Add To Selection from the Options bar. Click within each of the letters.

5 Add a new layer (Ctrl/Cmd+Shift+N), call it "Neon," and choose a vivid pink foreground color. Go to **Edit** > **Stroke**, using a stroke width of 10 pixels, and choose Center for Location. We can now drag the black-and-white layer to the trash can in the Layers palette.

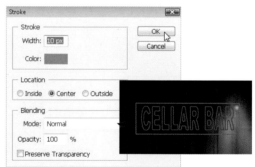

6 Choose the Rectangular Marquee tool and drag a selection around the lettering to form an outer border. Choose a bright orange color for the foreground and go to **Edit** > **Stroke**, using the same settings as before. Hit Ctrl/Cmd+D to deselect.

7 To fit the sign to the space above the door, go to **Edit** > **Transform** > **Distort**. Pull the corner handles on the bounding box around the lettering into the corners of the space. Take time to match the perspective by carefully adjusting each handle.

8 Use the Eraser tool to create small breaks in each letter. Ensure that these breaks have rounded ends to add to the realism of the neon tube effect. Now, choose the Brush tool and paint in the small prongs at right angles to these breaks in the lettering. Use a very small, hard brush and sample the color of the lettering with the Eyedropper tool. Repeat the same procedure in the border.

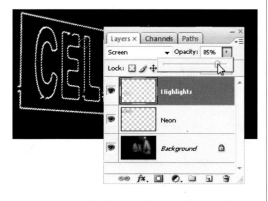

9 Ctrl/Cmd-click the Neon layer thumbnail in the Layers palette to select it, go to **Select > Modify > Contract**, and use a value of 2 pixels.

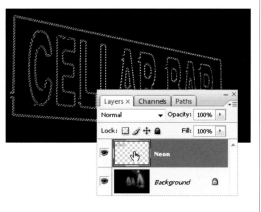

10 Add a new layer (Ctrl/Cmd+Shift+N), call it "Highlights," and use the Brush tool to paint white into the selection to create a highlight on the lettering.

Blur this a little with **Filter > Blur > Gaussian Blur,** using a very small blur radius. Set this layer's blending mode to Screen, reducing the opacity to 85%.

Tip

TRANSFORM COMMAND
To fit the sign to the available space, we've used the Transform > Distort command. Although Photoshop has a Perspective Transform command, the Distort tool allows us greater flexibility. Within the Transform function, you will see a bounding box surrounding the element on the layer. The element can be distorted geometrically by dragging the "handles" distributed around this box. You can skew the lettering by using the central handles on the top and bottom of the box.

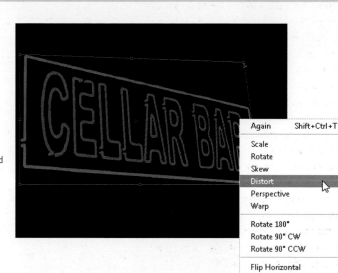

11 To create the neon glow, click the Neon layer and duplicate it (Ctrl/Cmd+J). Blur this layer with **Filter > Blur > Gaussian Blur**, using a Radius of 13.7. Duplicate the blurred layer, and set both of the blurred layers' blending modes to Screen. We can duplicate this layer a few more times to increase the glow amount.

12 To finish, choose the Brush tool and a soft brush. Brush some of the lettering color at a very low opacity along the top edge of the porch to indicate a reflected glow.

Creating a star-filled sky

Sometimes, a really good nighttime shot will be missing one vital component—the celestial majesty of a star-filled sky. Sadly, a cloudless night sky is not something that can always be relied on, but with the power of Photoshop at our fingertips, this is easily remedied.

The basic building blocks for the randomly placed stars are supplied by the Noise filter. This gives a random scattering of light-toned pixels that can be blurred and clumped together to create the starfield. We'll then add a simple moon and use a few basic layer blending modes to recreate that classic starry, starry night.

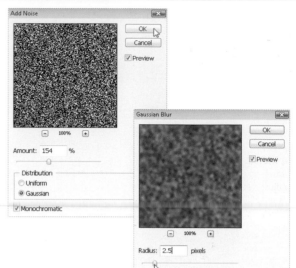

1 Open an appropriate nighttime image. Begin by adding a layer for the main collection of stars (Ctrl/Cmd+Shift+N). Call it "Stars," and fill it with black, using **Edit > Fill > Use: Black**.

2 Now, we'll apply some noise to this layer to create the foundation for the stars. Go to **Filter > Noise > Add Noise**. A fairly high level of noise is needed here, so drag the Amount slider up to 154%. Select Gaussian for Distribution and check the Monochrome box. Click OK to apply the noise. We need to blur this noise layer a little, so go to **Filter > Blur > Gaussian Blur**. Use a small value of about 2.5 pixels.

3 Before moving on, set the blending mode for the Stars layer to Screen. This will hide the black on the layer and leave just the white noise showing over the image. Don't worry that this layer doesn't look much like stars at the moment.

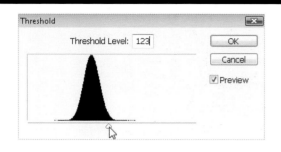

4 With the Stars layer still active, go to **Image > Adjustments > Threshold**. At the default Threshold value of 128, the stars already look pretty realistic, but we can modify the setting to fine-tune the density of the stars. By dragging the Threshold to the left (lowering the Threshold value), we can increase the density of the stars. Dragging it to the right decreases the number of stars. Here I've settled on a value of 123. Click OK.

6 Now, click again on the Stars layer and click the "Add layer mask" icon at the base of the Layers palette, to mask out the stars over the buildings. Click the Stars layer visibility eye to see the result.

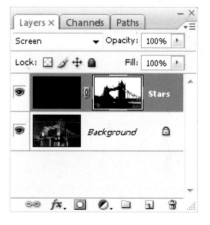

5 At this stage we need to add a Layer Mask to the Stars layer so that the stars are only visible in the sky, and not over the buildings. Hide the Stars layer temporarily, by clicking its visibility eye. Return to the background layer, choose the Eyedropper tool, and click anywhere in the dark blue of the sky. Go to **Select > Color Range** and drag the Fuzziness slider to 67 to select only the sky. Click OK.

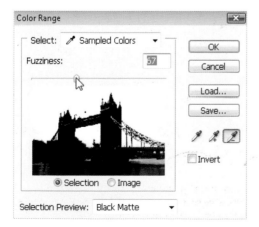

Tip

STARBURST BRUSH

Photoshop has a special brush that is useful for starfields. Using the Brush tool, click in the Brush Picker and choose the right-pointing arrow. Load the Assorted Brushes set from the list. Scroll down the Brush thumbnails and choose Starburst Small. You can now use this brush, with a very light yellow color, on the Extra Stars layer to add a touch of starlight twinkle!

LIGHTING EFFECTS

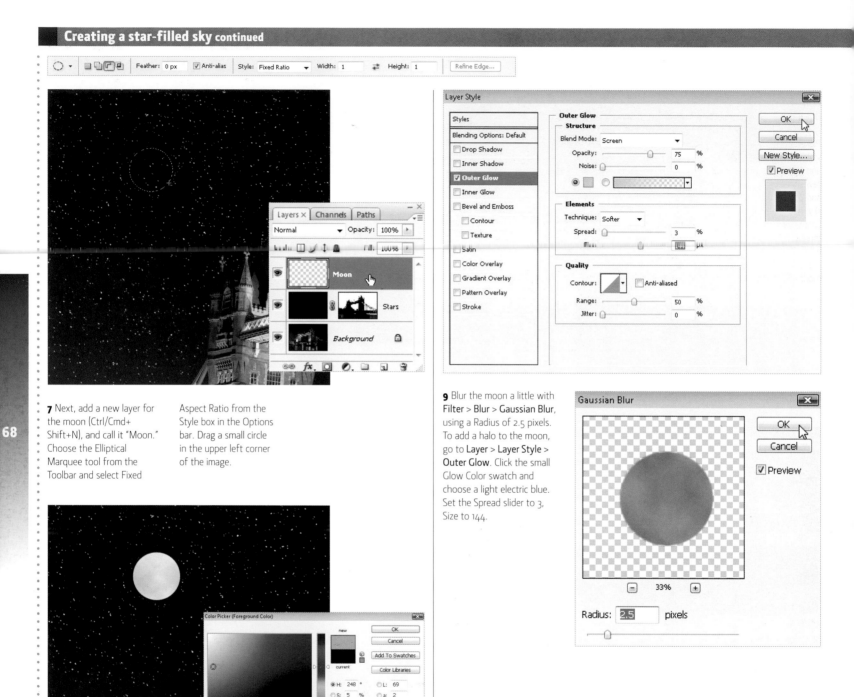

7 Next, add a new layer for the moon (Ctrl/Cmd+Shift+N), and call it "Moon." Choose the Elliptical Marquee tool from the Toolbar and select Fixed Aspect Ratio from the Style box in the Options bar. Drag a small circle in the upper left corner of the image.

8 Choose light blue/gray for the foreground color swatch, and a slightly darker shade for the background. Go to **Filter > Render > Clouds** to fill the moon, then use Ctrl/Cmd+D to deselect.

9 Blur the moon a little with **Filter > Blur > Gaussian Blur**, using a Radius of 2.5 pixels. To add a halo to the moon, go to **Layer > Layer Style > Outer Glow**. Click the small Glow Color swatch and choose a light electric blue. Set the Spread slider to 3, Size to 144.

68

10 Add another layer for some more stars, which we're going to add manually with a brush. Click on the Brush tool, and select a soft, 17-pixel brush from the Brush Picker. Choose a very light violet color for foreground, and with single clicks add a few softer, bigger stars here and there throughout the sky. Change the color to light yellow and add a few more stars. Blur these stars a little using Gaussian Blur and set the layer blending mode to Screen.

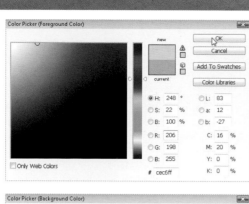

12 Finally, use the Eraser tool on the Stars layer to remove a few of the stars near the horizon, and on the Clouds layer to restrict the clouds to the area around the moon.

11 Add some very subtle clouds to the image. Create a final new layer, and call it "Clouds." Choose a vivid light blue for foreground and black for background. Fill this layer, using **Filter** > **Render** > **Clouds**. Blur the layer with **Filter** > **Blur** > **Gaussian Blur**, using a Radius of 34. Set the layer's blending mode to Soft Light, and the opacity to 42%.

Adding fire and flames

It's a natural phenomenon that has fascinated mankind since time immemorial. Fire! There are a few, sadly rather expensive plug-ins that can be used with Photoshop to recreate fire and flames, but here we'll look at a technique using Photoshop exclusively, without any add-ons.

The most difficult aspect of recreating fire is its essentially random quality. For this, we'll use the Clouds filter as a starting point, which has a great degree of randomness built in. Color is all-important when it comes to fire, so we'll use a customized Gradient Map to add this vital component.

So, fire up Photoshop, and feel the heat!

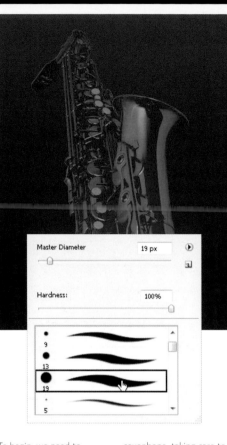

1 To begin, we need to isolate the saxophone from its background. Hit Q on the keyboard to enter Quick Mask mode, choose the Brush tool and paint with black over the entire saxophone, taking care to follow the edges precisely. This will result in the whole object being covered with the red Quick Mask. Now hit Q again, to exit the mode and generate a selection.

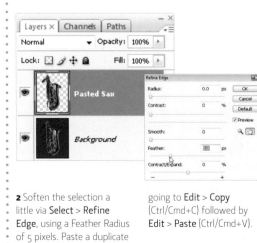

2 Soften the selection a little via **Select > Refine Edge**, using a Feather Radius of 5 pixels. Paste a duplicate copy of the instrument by going to **Edit > Copy** (Ctrl/Cmd+C) followed by **Edit > Paste** (Ctrl/Cmd+V).

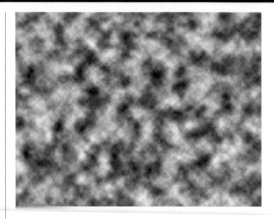

3 Add a new layer (Ctrl/Cmd+Shift+N) for the first fire layer. Hit D on the keyboard to reset the swatch colors to default foreground/background colors and go to **Filter > Render > Clouds**. This will fill the layer with a random Clouds fill, which is a good basis for the fire effect.

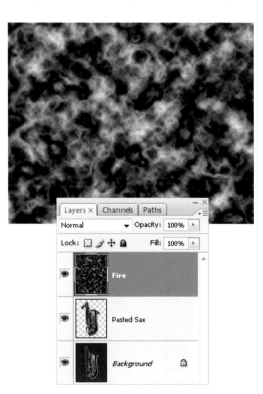

4 To make this layer look a little more like raging fire, go to **Filter > Render > Difference Clouds**. This action needs to be repeated two or three times. To reapply this filter, simply return to the Filter menu and Difference Clouds will be the first entry (or hit Ctrl/Cmd+F). In the screenshot, the filter has been applied three times.

5 To color the fire, go to **Layer > New Adjustment Layer > Gradient Map**. Click OK. In the Gradient Map dialog box, click in the Gradient swatch to invoke the Gradient Editor. Double-click the left-hand color stop below the gradient ramp and choose a rich, dark brown from the picker. Next, double-click the right-hand color stop and choose a bright yellow. Click on the midpoint color stop between these two, then click off to add another color stop, choosing a vivid red by clicking in the color swatch. Grab each stop in turn, moving them roughly into the positions shown in the screenshot. Click OK. The layer will now look much more like fire.

6 Go to **Layer > Merge Down** to merge the Gradient Map layer with the clouds layer. Now zoom out of the image a little and go to **Edit > Transform > Scale**. Grab the top handle on the Transform bounding box and drag it upward,

stretching the flames layer. Click the commit checkmark in the Options bar to apply the transformation. Click on the Crop tool, select the entire image, and apply the crop. This deletes the invisible stretched flames.

7 Change the blending mode for this Fire layer to Screen. Blur the fire a little using **Filter > Blur > Motion Blur**. Choose an Angle of 90 degrees and a Distance of 50 pixels.

8 Add a layer mask to the fire layer using **Layer > Layer Mask > Reveal All**. Choose the Brush tool and select a soft-edged, round brush from the Brush Picker. Increase the size of the brush with the right-facing bracket key (]) on the keyboard and paint out the top of the flames with black, varying the opacity as you go. Painting black onto the mask will hide this area of flames. After masking, right-click/Ctrl-click the thumbnail for the layer mask and choose Apply Layer Mask.

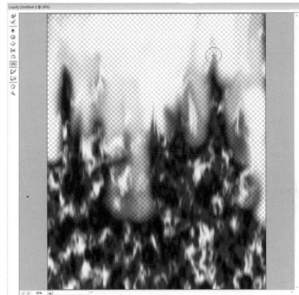

9 To make the flames appear to lick around the saxophone, use the Liquify command. Go to **Filter > Liquify**. Although the Liquify dialog box looks very complicated, we'll use it here in a very simple way. Choose the Turbulence tool from the tools on the left, and set the Turbulence jitter slider to 64%. Use the brush at a fairly large size to drag a few flame tips upward. Just click and drag on the flame tips. Click OK to apply the Liquify results.

Adding fire and flames continued

10 For more impact, add a major league fireball behind the saxophone. Click on the original background layer and add a new layer (Ctrl/Cmd+Shift+N), naming it "Fireball." Choose the Lasso tool from the Toolbar and draw an irregularly shaped selection in the top two-thirds of the canvas. Choose red as the foreground color and bright yellow for the background. Then go to **Filter > Render > Clouds.**

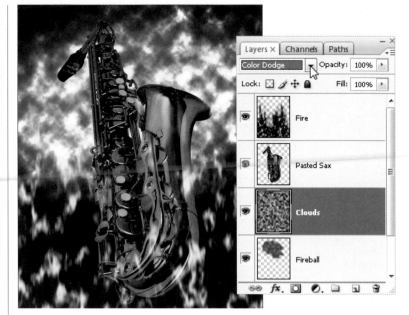

11 Hit Ctrl/Cmd+D to deselect, then blur this shape using **Filter > Blur > Gaussian Blur.** Use a Blur Radius of 55 pixels.

12 Now add some turbulence to the fireball. Create another new layer (Ctrl/Cmd+Shift+N) and hit D on the keyboard to revert to default black/white colors. Return to **Filter > Render > Clouds** and apply the filter. Set the blending mode for this layer to Color Dodge.

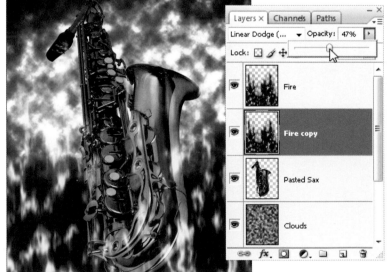

13 Click on the Fire layer and duplicate it (Ctrl/Cmd+J). Drag this second fire layer below the first in the Layers palette and go to **Filter > Blur > Motion Blur.** Use an Angle of 90 degrees and a Distance of 460 pixels. Set the blending mode for this layer to Linear Dodge and reduce the opacity to 47%.

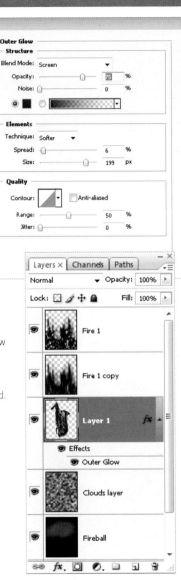

14 Return to the Fireball layer and add an Outer Glow layer style, using **Layer > Layer Style > Outer Glow**. Click in the Glow Color swatch, choosing a vivid red. Set the Spread slider to 6 and the Size to 199.

Simulating candlelight

Candlelight has unique properties and is the very essence of romantic, atmospheric still-life studies. Unfortunately it's notoriously difficult to photograph successfully. Fortunately, Photoshop supplies us with all of the tools that we need to simulate stunningly convincing candlelight effects. Here, we'll begin by using the powerful Lighting Effects filter to set the scene. The essential extras for the candlelight are supplied by simple gradients and layer blending modes.

1 To begin, we need to adjust the overall lighting in the image. To simulate authentic candlelit conditions, we need a single diffused pool of light that illuminates just one area of the scene. Duplicate the background layer (Ctrl/Cmd+J) and call it "Lighting Effects."

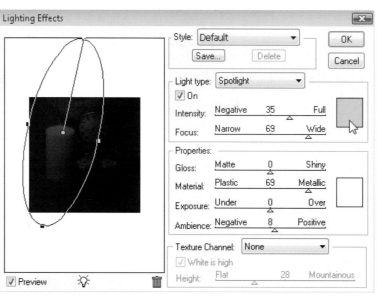

2 Open the Lighting Effects dialog (**Filter > Render > Lighting Effects**). Click the light color swatch in the Light Type category, choosing a mid yellow color from the picker. In the Style box, choose Default. In the Preview pane, grab the spot in the very center of the light pool and drag it so that it sits at the top of the candle. Drag the light pool handle that sits in the bottom right of the image thumbnail and rotate the pool counter-clockwise until this handle is at the one o'clock position. Now, drag this handle upwards so that it just disappears from view.

3 To enlarge the light pool, drag the left hand side handle outwards. Set the Intensity slider to 53, and Ambience to 10. Click OK, bearing in mind this filter can take a while to apply.

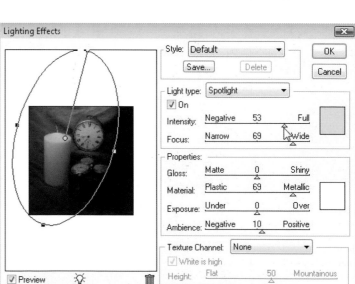

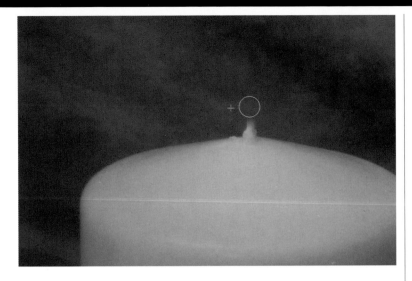

4 Choose the Clone Stamp tool and clone out most of the candle wick. Simply position the tool next to the wick, hold down the Alt key and click to sample. Then, click over the wick.

5 Light from a candle flame travels through the actual body of the candle, so select the top half of the candle. Switch to Quick Mask mode (Q) and paint the mask over the candle with a hard edged brush. When the mask is complete hit Q again to exit quick mask. Now, go to **Select** > **Refine Edge** and use a Feather Radius of 5 pixels

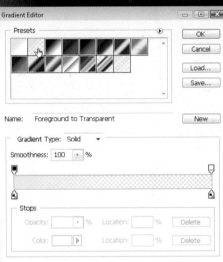

6 Add a new layer, and choose a bright yellow for the foreground color. Choose the Gradient tool, click in the Gradient Picker and select Foreground to Transparent from the swatches. Now, click and drag the Gradient tool vertically across the selection.

7 Hit Ctrl/Cmd+D to deselect and go to **Filter** > **Blur** > **Gaussian Blur** using a radius of 8 pixels. Change the blending mode for this layer to Screen, reducing the opacity a little.

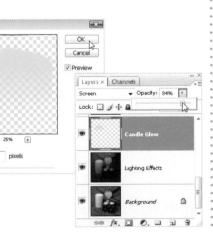

Simulating candlelight continued

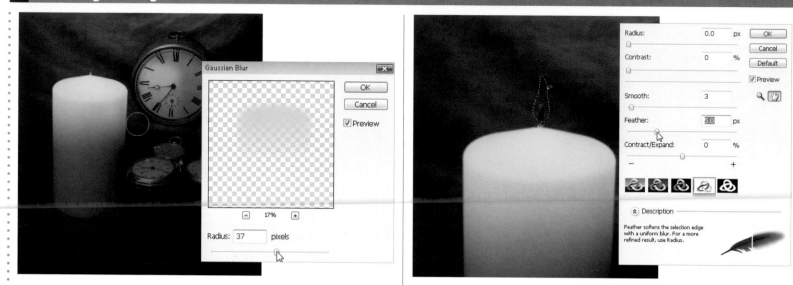

8 Duplicate this layer (Ctrl/Cmd+J) and move the copy so that it sits over the left half of the clock face. Blur this layer further via **Filter > Blur > Gaussian Blur**, using a 37 pixel Radius. Set the blending mode for this layer to Overlay. Now, use the Eraser tool to erase the parts of this layer which are outside the clock face.

10 Hit L on the keyboard to activate the Lasso tool and add a new layer. With this tool, draw a simple flame shape over the wick. Feather this selection via **Selection > Refine Edge**, using a Radius of 5 pixels.

9 Choose the Brush tool, and add a new layer. Click the Foreground color swatch, choosing a deep brown from the picker. Now, paint a short wick onto the candle. Set the blending mode for this layer to Dissolve to create a broken edge to the wick.

11 Select the Brush tool, choosing a very light yellow for the Foreground color and a soft brush from the Brush Picker. Reduce the Brush Opacity to 40% in the Options bar and paint within the selection. After filling the selection, paint again at the top of the flame to intensify the color. Reduce the size of the brush, choose white and paint some small white streaks within the flame. Deselect (Ctrl/Cmd+D) and go to **Filter > Blur > Motion Blur**. Choose 90 degrees for Angle and 65 for distance. Click OK and set the layer blending mode to Screen.

12 Change back to yellow and return to the candle glow layer. Increase the brush size to approximately 700 pixels and, with a single click, place a soft glow over the candle flame.

13 Finally, choose a warm orange color, reduce the size of the brush, and add a new layer, setting the blending mode to Overlay. Paint with this brush at low opacity over a few parts of the watches which are closest to the candlelight. Also paint with this brush around the left-hand side of the clock case.

DODGE TOOL

When the image is complete, you can use the Dodge tool on the Lighting Effects layer to selectively lighten parts of the image nearest the candlelight. This will give the effect of bright accents and highlights here and there. To use this tool, select it from the Toolbar (it may be nested below the Burn tool) and set the Exposure to just 7% in the Options bar. Set the Range to midtones and choose a small brush size. Then carefully add subtle lighting to small areas.

Stage Lighting

Some of the most creative lighting in the world can be seen in the theater. Stage lighting truly is an art form in its own right, and thanks to the wonder of Photoshop CS3, you too can "paint with light" in a creative and dramatic way.

In this recipe, we're going to use the wonderfully powerful Lighting Effects filter, but, thanks to the capabilities of CS3, we're going to use it in a uniquely flexible way, namely by using Smart Filters. Smart Filters allow you to use conventional Photoshop Filters in an endlessly re-editable way. Once you've converted a layer to a Smart Object and applied a filter, you can modify that filter effect as many times as you like simply by double-clicking its entry in the Layers palette.

We'll top the whole effect off by adding lens flare—representing another stage light—to superb effect. So, if you fancy a little theater lighting, this project is for you. Sit back and marvel at the power of Smart Filters!

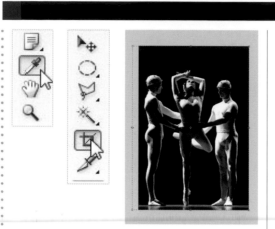

1 Open the start image and choose the Eyedropper tool. Click in the background area next to the left-hand figure in the image to sample the color. Hit X on the keyboard to swap the Foreground and Background colors. Now, choose the Crop tool and drag a crop box around the entire image. Grab the far left center handle and drag it to the left to even up the distances between the two outer figures and the edges of the image. Double-click within the image to crop.

2 Duplicate the Background Layer (Ctrl/Cmd+J), and name this layer "Lighting." We'll use the Lighting Effects filter here, but we want to use it as a Smart Filter, so first go to **Filter > Convert For Smart Filters**. You'll see the Smart Object icon appear on the layer thumbnail within the Layers palette.

3 Go to **Filter > Render > Lighting Effects**. In the Lighting Effects dialog, click in the Style box and choose Triple Spotlight from the list. In the Preview pane you'll now see three dots. These dots represent the center point for each light pool. Start by positioning each of these dots over the waistlines of the three dancers.

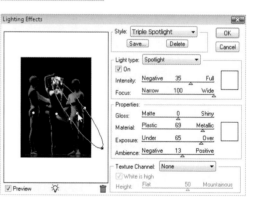

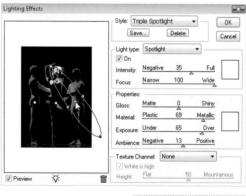

4 Now, click on the center dot for the right-hand light. Click on the color swatch in the Light Type and choose a vivid red from the Color Picker. Then, click the far left-hand spot and choose a vivid blue.

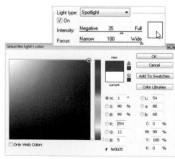

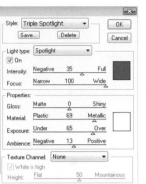

5 You can adjust the size and direction of each of the light pools by dragging on the handles around them. You can rotate the pool by dragging on the handle at the end of the bisecting line. Use the screenshot as a guide for positioning.

6 Control the brightness of each light by clicking on its center spot and adjusting the Intensity slider. Adjust the width and range of the light beam with the Focus slider. The Focus needs to be wide enough so that the side lights are reflected on the central figure.

7 Add a new layer (Ctrl/Cmd+Shift+N). We're going to add a lens flare effect to the central figure, so fill this new layer with black, via **Edit > Fill**, choosing Black for Contents. Now, so that you can use Smart Filters again, go to **Filter > Convert For Smart Filters**.

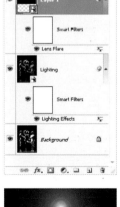

8 Go to **Filter > Render > Lens Flare**. Choose the 50-300mm Zoom. Drag the Brightness slider to 120%. Drag the crosshairs for the flare center roughly into the center of the Preview pane. Click OK to apply. Set this layer to Screen blending mode. Adjust the intensity of the lens flare simply by reducing the layer's opacity.

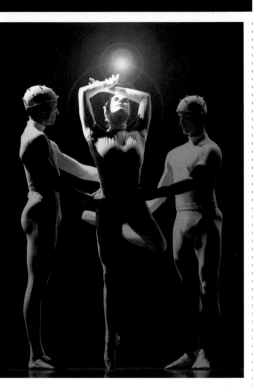

9 It's always a good idea to save a version via **File > Save As**, saving the image as a PSD file. This lets you keep the layers so you can go back and re-edit the filters if you like. When you're done, you can flatten the image via **Layer > Flatten Image**.

Tip

FLARE COLORS

You can adjust the Hue and intensity of the colors contained within the Lens Flare by using Image > Adjustments > Hue/Saturation on the flare layer. In the Hue/Saturation dialog box, adjust the Hue slider to change the actual colors in the flare. Drag the Saturation slider to the right to intensify them, and to the left to reduce their intensity.

Chiaroscuro

Chiaroscuro, literally translated as "light and dark," is a technique of pictorial representation most associated with great artists such as Rembrandt and Caravaggio. It's true that a similar effect could be created in the photographic studio with the careful use of studio lighting. Sadly, not all of us have such equipment, or the knowledge needed to organize such complicated lighting, and besides, the results in camera can still lack depth and creativity.

By simulating this classic technique in Photoshop, we're allowed much more control over which parts of the image fade into darkness, and which parts are blessed with the scintillating, jewel-like highlights so typical of the technique. Key to this Photoshop technique is the use of a layer filled with 50% gray; a pure neutral in digital imaging terms. By setting this layer to Overlay and painting onto it with black or white, the tones within the image can be very accurately controlled and modified.

For a stunning image, follow the recipe and take a trip into the dark side of light! For the initial image sharpening here, we'll employ the wonder of Smart Filters, so you can readjust the sharpening whenever you want to.

1 We'll sharpen the image with a Smart Filter, so we can always go back and modify the sharpening later. Start by going to **Filter > Convert For** Smart Filters. Go to **Filter > Sharpen > Unsharp Mask** and use these settings: Amount 99, Radius 4.1, Threshold 5.

3 Click the adjustment layer icon at the bottom of the Layers palette and choose Solid Color. Choose a very dark tan color for the fill and click OK. Set the layer blending mode to Soft Light and reduce the opacity to 22%.

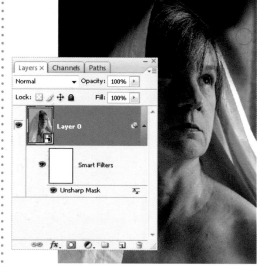

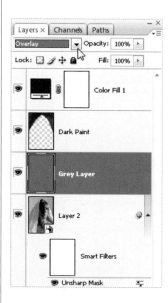

2 Add a new layer to the image (Ctrl/Cmd+Shift+N), set the blending mode for this layer to Multiply and choose the Brush tool. Choose a large soft brush from the Brush picker, and choose a very dark brown color from the Color palette. Paint around the head with this brush to conceal the background behind the main subject. Paint over the edges of the veil a little, at very low opacity.

4 Now, to begin creating the dramatic tones in the image, click on the background layer and then select **Layer > New > Layer**. Go to **Edit > Fill** and choose 50% Gray from the Contents box. Set the blending mode for this layer to Overlay, and call it "Gray Layer." By painting onto this layer with black and white, we can selectively darken and lighten the image tones.

5 Ensure that black is your foreground color and choose the Brush tool. Using a soft brush, paint at very low opacity (13%) over the shaded side of the face and veil. As you paint, the tones in this area will darken. Concentrate on the areas of dark and midtones.

6 We need to create some really dramatic darks here, taking the darkest tones down to almost black. The more you paint over the tones on this layer, the darker they will become. Increase the size of the brush with the square bracket keys on the keyboard and paint over the chest area.

7 Now, concentrate on the midtones on the lighter side of the face. Using the brush at a fairly small size, gently paint over these areas with black to increase the contrast between these areas and the lightest tones.

8 We want to introduce a little color into the image to help give it an aged effect. Add a new layer and set the blending mode to Color. Choose a mid tan from the color palette and paint with this color here and there throughout the image. Use the brush at low opacity, building the depth of color up gradually.

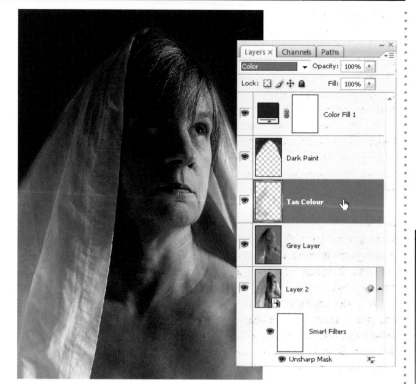

9 Return to the Background Layer and add a Hue/Saturation adjustment layer via **Layer** > **New Adjustment Layer** > **Hue/Saturation**. We need to make a subtle change to the hue and desaturate the image slightly, so use these settings in the dialog: Hue +4, Saturation −24, Lightness −6.

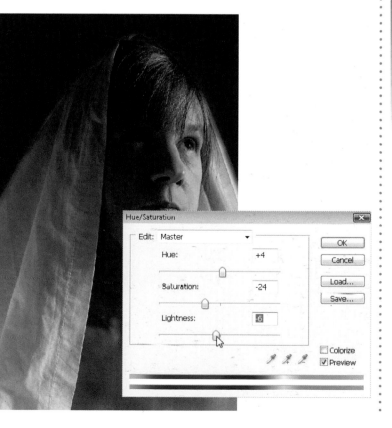

Chiaroscuro continued

10 This adjustment layer has a layer mask attached to it, allowing us to hide parts of the layer. Paint with black on to the lighter side of the face and veil to reveal a little of the color from the underlying background layer.

11 We need to selectively boost the highlights on the image to add some sparkle, so return to the 50% gray layer. This time, we need to paint with white onto this layer to lighten tones. Ensure that the foreground color is white and begin to paint over the lightest tones in the face.

13 Add a final new layer at the top of the layer stack and set the blending mode to Multiply. Hit D on the keyboard so your foreground color is black, increase the brush size and paint black onto this layer over the back edge of the veil. Use the brush at 35% opacity. This will soften the transition between the background and figure.

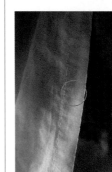

14 Reduce the brush opacity even further in the Options bar and paint black very gently over the other dark areas in the image.

82

Tip

FEEL THE PRESSURE

For a project such as this, it's a great advantage to use a pressure-sensitive graphics tablet instead of a standard mouse. The brushes in Photoshop can be modified to react to the pressure capabilities of a graphics tablet, and this makes controlling the opacity of a brush much more successful than using the Opacity slider in the Options bar.

To set these pressure capabilities, hit F5 on the keyboard to display the Brush Options palette, and choose the Other Dynamics category. From the Opacity Jitter Control box choose Pen Pressure. Now, when you're using the Brush tool, the more pressure you apply to your stylus, the more opaque the brush stroke will be.

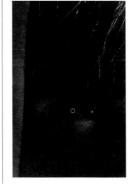

12 Use the brush at a very small size and a very low opacity of just 10%. Try to pick out sparkling highlights and edges with the brush, paying special attention to the lighter parts in and around the eyes. Now, increase the size of the brush and gently brush over the lightest areas in the shadow side of the face, including the white of the eye.

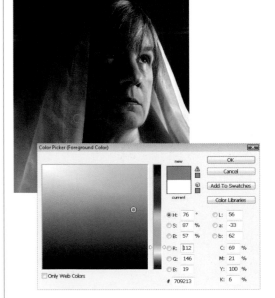

15 To increase the aged appearance, double-click the Solid Color adjustment layer and choose a vivid midrange green. On the adjustment layer's mask, paint over the lightest parts of the image with black. This will hide the green fill in these areas.

16 Now we'll add a texture to the image, for a more authentic look. Click on the top layer in the Layers palette and go to **Layer > New Fill Layer > Pattern**. Hit OK and, in the following Pattern Fill dialog, click on the Pattern swatch. Choose the right-pointing arrow, and select Artists Surfaces. Choose Canvas from the thumbnails. Increase the Scale slider to 496%. Set the blending mode for this layer to Multiply, Opacity 55%.

17 Finally, return to the 50% Gray Fill layer and use white to brush in just the suggestion of a teardrop on the lower eyelid. Use a hard brush at 50% opacity for this.

You can now double-click the entry for the Unsharp Mask Smart Filter in the Layers palette and adjust the sharpness of the base layer to your own taste.

NATURAL WORLD EFFECTS

Summer to Autumn

Nothing quite compares with the colors of trees in autumn, but sadly, we're not always guaranteed the weather to get one of those classic autumn shots. As ever, Photoshop comes to the rescue! In this recipe, we're going to perform some weather alchemy, turning a vibrant green landscape into a scene resplendent in shades of gold and russet. We'll start by using a couple of Color Balance adjustment layers to change the initial hues, and we'll restrict the placement of these colors with layer masks. For a touch of subtlety, we'll use Photoshop CS3's new Lighter Color blending mode.

Making selections is never simple, but thanks to CS3's brand new Quick Selection Tool and the Refine Edge command, we can easily make complicated selections. So, to renew your memories of the season of mists and mellow fruitfulness, fire up Photoshop, and start adjusting those colors!

1 Open the start image and duplicate the Background Layer (Ctrl/ Cmd+J). Go to **Layer > New Adjustment Layer > Color Balance**. In the Color Balance dialog, ensure that the Preview box is checked so you can see the effect as you make the adjustments. Click on the Midtones button. Now, grab the Cyan/Red slider and drag it to +66.

2 Select the Magenta/Green slider and drag it to the left, to a value of -14. Drag the Yellow/Blue slider to the left, to a value of -81.8.

3 Click on the layer mask associated with the adjustment layer in the Layers palette and go to **Edit > Fill**, choosing Black for Contents. This will hide the effect with a mask. Change the blending mode for this layer to Lighter Color. Choose the Brush tool and ensure that your foreground color is white. Click in the Brush Picker and choose a soft, round brush. If you're using a graphics tablet, open Brush Options (F5), and ensure Shape Dynamics is not checked.

4 Using the brush at 75% opacity, begin to paint with white over the trees, to reveal the modified colors. Use the brush at a suitable size for any small trees, and at a larger size over broad areas. If you paint over a building by mistake, simply change your foreground color to black and paint back into the image to remove the color.

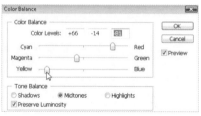

5 Time for another color change. This time we're going to adjust the lighter areas in the foliage, so again, go to **Layer > New Adjustment Layer > Color Balance**. Click on the Highlights button and drag the Cyan/Red slider to the right, to a value of +53. Drag the Yellow/Blue slider to the left to a value of -60. Again, set the blending mode to Lighter Color, and fill the mask with black via **Edit > Fill**, choosing Black for Contents.

6 Using the same brush at a smaller size, you can paint with white over parts of the trees to add some gold and brown highlights here and there. This can be quite a laborious process, but it's worth taking your time. By using the brush at a fairly low opacity, you can slowly build up these tones simply by working over certain areas repeatedly.

7 The overall intensity of these golden areas can be reduced by modifying the opacity of the adjustment layer in the Layers palette. This applies to both of the adjustment layers we've made.

9 We need to darken the foreground, so choose the Quick Selection tool from the Toolbar. In the Options bar, check the Auto Enhance box. Click on the Background Layer and drag the tool over the grassy foreground area. Now, go to **Layer** > **New** > **Layer Via Copy**. This will paste a copy of the foreground area into a new layer.

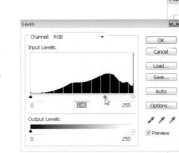

10 Go to **Image** > **Adjustments** > **Levels**. Grab the midpoint slider and drag it to the right, to an Input Level of 0.46. Click OK. Now go to **Image** > **Adjustments** > **Hue/Saturation**. Drag the Saturation slider to the left, to a value of -60.

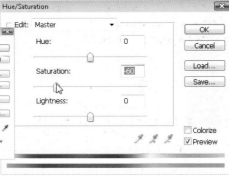

87

8 Add a new layer (Ctrl/Cmd+Shift+N), naming it "Sky Gradient." Choose the Gradient tool from the Toolbar and click the Foreground color swatch. Choose a middle gray from the color picker. In the Gradient Picker, choose Foreground To Transparent. In the Options bar, choose Linear Gradient. Click and hold with the Gradient tool in the middle of the sky and drag a gradient down to about the bottom of the church. Release the mouse button.

Simulating rain

Hands up, anyone who wants to stand in the rain on a cold gray day with an expensive digital camera! No takers? It's hardly surprising—there are some aspects of nature that we may wish to capture on camera, but without enduring the misery of the actual experience. Rain isn't difficult to simulate in Photoshop. The Noise filter plays a major role in the process, providing exactly the kind of random factor that this subject demands. The part of the wind, driving the rain across the image, is played by the Motion Blur filter, and a simple layer blending mode adds the required subtlety.

1 Open a suitable image for the rain treatment. Hit Ctrl/Cmd+D on the keyboard to revert to default foreground and background colors. Add a new layer (Ctrl/Cmd+ Shift+N), call it "Rain Layer," and fill it with white using **Edit > Fill > Use: White**. Go to **Filter > Noise > Add Noise**. Use an Amount of 95, Uniform and Monochromatic.

2 The noise is a bit too dense, so go to **Image > Adjustments > Levels**. Drag the Black Point slider to the right until the Input Value reads 71. This will increase the contrast of the Noise layer and thin out the speckles.

3 Blur this Noise layer a little with **Filter > Blur > Gaussian Blur**, using a Radius value of 0.5 pixels. To add the effect of driving rain, go to **Filter > Blur > Motion Blur**, choosing an Angle of 63 and a Distance of 49 pixels.

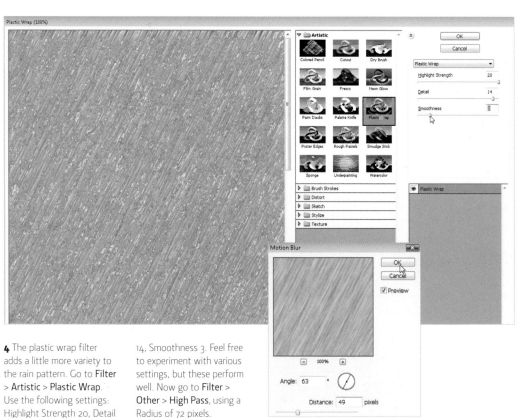

4 The plastic wrap filter adds a little more variety to the rain pattern. Go to **Filter > Artistic > Plastic Wrap**. Use the following settings: Highlight Strength 20, Detail 14, Smoothness 3. Feel free to experiment with various settings, but these perform well. Now go to **Filter > Other > High Pass**, using a Radius of 72 pixels.

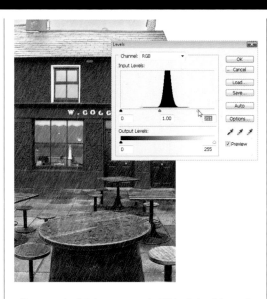

9 Set the Reflections layer blending mode to Soft Light. Choose the Eraser tool and erase any parts of this layer that sit on top of the furniture in the foreground. Flatten the image using **Layer > Flatten Image**.

5 Re-apply the Motion Blur filter, with the settings from the previous step, and set the blending mode for the Rain layer to Hard Light.

7 Return to the Rain layer and go to **Image > Adjustments > Levels**. Drag the White Point slider to the left a little to increase the brightness of the rain itself.

6 Click on the background layer and go to **Layer > New Adjustment Layer > Levels** and click OK. We need to darken the image a little to intensify the Rain layer, so drag the midpoint slider to the right a little.

8 For the reflections, choose the Rectangular Marquee tool and click on the background layer. Drag a selection over the very bottom of the building. Right-click/Ctrl-click within the selection with the Marquee tool, and choose Layer Via Copy. Now go to **Edit > Transform > Flip Vertical**. Use the Move tool to drag the Reflections layer down so that it sits on the paving in front of the building.

Tip

RE-EDITING ADJUSTMENT LAYERS

The reason we use adjustment layers to make Levels or Curves adjustments is that they can easily be readjusted at any time during the image-making process. To modify a Levels adjustment layer, simply double-click its thumbnail in the Layers palette to invoke the Levels dialog box. Make your alteration to the Levels value and click OK.

Adding water droplets

The classic image of a flower or some foliage glistening with drops of dew can be very difficult to capture. Not only is this photo opportunity one that requires the photographer to be in the right place at the right time, but finding that place demands early-morning forays out with camera in hand. For the digital photographer who is more of a late riser, Photoshop once again comes to the rescue. The process of creating digital dewdrops involves making simple elliptical selections, using the Spherize filter, and then calling on Layer Styles for a little help with the final effect. Twinkling highlights are added courtesy of the Gradient tool.

1 Open the original image and select the Elliptical Marquee tool from the Toolbar. Ensure that the Add to Selection icon is active in the Options bar. Drag two overlapping elliptical selections near the middle of the leaf to generate the water droplets.

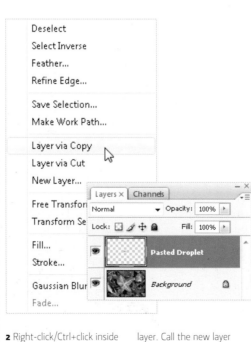

2 Right-click/Ctrl+click inside the active selection and choose Layer Via Copy. This will paste the selected part of the leaf onto a new layer. Call the new layer "Pasted Droplet."

3 Right-click/Ctrl+click the Pasted Droplet layer thumbnail and choose Select Layer Transparency. Now, with the selection active, go to **Filter > Distort >** **Spherize**. Use an amount of 100% and set the Mode to Normal. Click OK and go to **Filter > Spherize** to reapply the filter (or hit Ctrl/Cmd+F).

4 To create a subtle shadow, duplicate the Pasted Droplet layer (Ctrl/Cmd+J) and Ctrl/Cmd-click this new layer thumbnail to generate a selection from its transparency. Ensure that black is the foreground color and go to **Edit > Fill**. Choose Foreground Color from the Contents box and hit OK. Ctrl/Cmd+D to deselect.

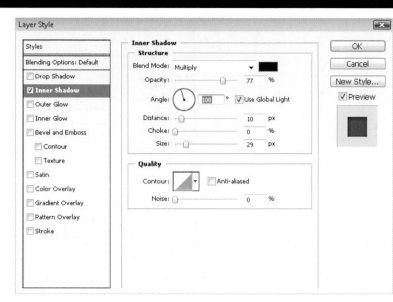

Tip

MANUALLY DRAWING
SELECTIONS FOR
FREEHAND SHAPED
DROPLETS
You may prefer your
water droplets to have a
less regular and more
organic shape. In this
case, instead of drawing
the initial droplet
selection with the
Elliptical Marquee tool in
Step 1, try drawing a
freehand shape for the
drops with the Lasso tool.
Remember to close your
selection by returning to
your starting point and
clicking with the tool.

8 Click and drag a gradient
vertically over the active
selection. Hit Ctrl/Cmd+D to
deselect. To blur this
highlight a little, go to **Filter
> Blur > Gaussian Blur**. Use
a Blur Radius of 0.7 pixels.

9 Add a final layer and
draw a very small elliptical
selection at the end of the
droplet. Fill this selection
with white using **Edit >
Fill**. Blur the layer with
Gaussian Blur, using a
Radius sufficient to
disguise the hard edge.
Here I've used 3.7 pixels.

10 Using the above method,
you can add as many
droplets as you wish,
although the best effect is
achieved with just a few.

5 Hit Ctrl/Cmd+[to move
this layer one position down
the stack. Now, blur it with
Filter > Blur > Gaussian Blur,
using a Blur Radius of 10
pixels. Use the Move tool to
move it down and to the
right so it creates a shadow
for the droplet. Set the
blending mode to Darken
and reduce opacity to 57%.

6 To create the shadow
inside the droplet, click on
the top layer and go to
**Layer > Layer Style > Inner
Shadow**. In the Layer Styles
panel, set the opacity to
77%, Distance to 10 pixels,
Size to 29 pixels. For Angle,
choose 108.

7 Add a new layer (Ctrl/
Cmd+Shift+N) and call it
"Reflections." With the
Elliptical Marquee tool, drag
an elongated ellipse across
the largest of the two
droplets. Ensure that the
foreground color is white,
and choose the Gradient
tool. Choose Foreground to
Transparent from the
Gradient Picker, and Linear
Gradient from the Toolbar.

91

Adding rainbows

Of all weather phenomena, rainbows are the most beautiful and colorful, and carry the mythical promise of pots of gold. Unfortunately, capturing a rainbow with a camera requires a huge amount of luck—it's another classic example of the right-time, right-place school of photography. Luckily, with Photoshop, it's not difficult to add a rainbow to an image after the fact.

In this example, we'll use the Gradient tool, which includes a ready-made rainbow gradient. To get more realistic results, we'll use the rainbow gradient in conjunction with a black-to-transparent gradient.

So, no more chasing rainbows—it's Photoshop to the rescue!

1 The ideal candidate for a rainbow effect is an image that has a dark, dramatic sky, contrasted with shafts of sunlight.

2 Begin by adding a new layer to the image (Ctrl/Cmd+Shift+N), and call it "Rainbow." This will help us position the finished rainbow. Now choose the Gradient tool from the Toolbar. Click in the Gradient Picker in the Options bar.

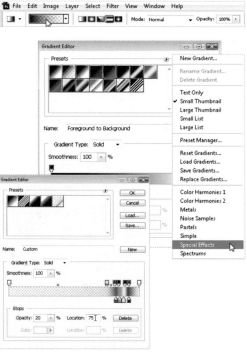

3 Click the small, right-pointing arrow in the top right of the Gradient Picker and choose Special Effects. Click OK. From the Gradient Swatches, choose Russell's Rainbow. Click on the light gray Opacity Stop on the upper edge of the gradient band and enter 75 in the Location box.

4 Choose Radial Gradient from the Options bar, and, with the blank layer active in the Layers palette, position the mouse pointer on the horizon line and click and drag a gradient from the center of the image toward the right-hand edge. Release the mouse button at the tree near the edge of the image.

5 Choose the Move tool and drag the rainbow into position, just past the center of the image. If the rainbow needs to be resized, ensure Show Transform Controls is checked in the Options bar and resize the rainbow using the bounding box corner handles. Remember to hold down the Shift key to retain the proportions. Set the blending mode for this layer to Screen.

6 Go to **Filter** > **Blur** > **Gaussian Blur** and set the Radius slider value to 60 pixels.

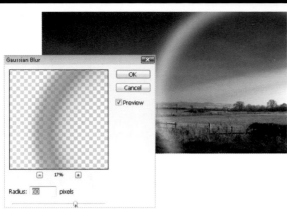

7 Hit D on the keyboard to revert to default foreground/background colors and choose the Gradient tool again. Click the Gradient Picker to bring up the Gradient Editor. Click the small black arrow, choose Reset Gradients, and click OK. Choose Foreground to Transparent in the Gradient Picker.

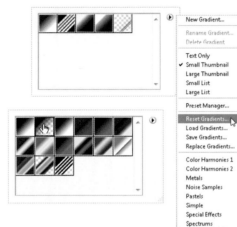

8 Choose Linear Gradient in the Options bar and click and drag a gradient from the bottom to the top of the entire image. Clean up any parts of the rainbow that project over the land with the Eraser tool.

9 To add some intensity to the rainbow, duplicate this layer (Ctrl/Cmd+J), setting the opacity for the new layer to 40%.

10 For a subtle double rainbow effect, duplicate this layer again and move it to the left with the Move tool. Re-apply the Gaussian Blur filter. (This can be done quickly by going to the Filter menu and clicking on the first entry, or hitting Ctrl/Cmd+F.) Apply this filter again if necessary to render this second rainbow only just visible. Again, use the Eraser tool to clean up any unwanted rainbow effect.

Simulating lightning

Catching real lightning with a compact digital camera can be a difficult and somewhat dangerous activity. The choice is either to spend a great deal of time outside in a storm waiting for the perfect moment, or a great deal of money on special photographic equipment.

Although we can't replicate the roar of thunder in Photoshop, we can easily add realistic lightning effects to photographic images. Of course, we could just draw a lightning bolt with a brush and apply a little glow to the layer, but that's unlikely to resemble the random qualities of real lightning. Instead, in this example, we'll use the Clouds filter and a simple gradient to convincingly imitate Mother Nature. The effect is positively electrifying.

1 This image certainly has the potential to be stormy, but let's start by adding a little more drama before we create the lightning. Add a new layer (Ctrl/Cmd+Shift+N), call it "Sky Gradient," and choose a dark blue/black for the foreground color. Choose the Gradient tool from the Toolbar. Select Foreground to Background from the Gradient Picker, and Linear Gradient from the Options bar. Drag a gradient from the top to the bottom of the image. Set the layer blend mode to Multiply and reduce opacity to 60%.

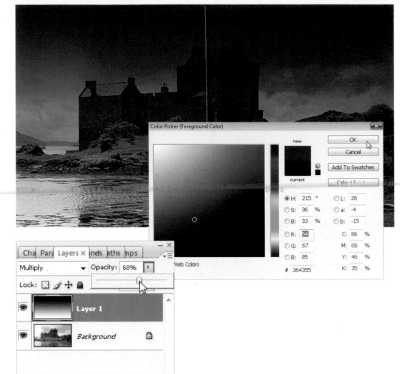

2 Stay with the Gradient tool and add another new layer (Ctrl/Cmd+Shift+N), calling it "Lightning." Choose Foreground to Background from the Gradient Picker and hit D on the keyboard to revert to default black/white swatches. Drag a short gradient diagonally across the central tower of the castle.

3 Now go to **Filter > Render > Difference Clouds**. A dark jagged band will appear across the diagonal center of the layer. Go to **Image > Adjustments > Levels** and drag the middle slider below the histogram to the left until the lightning bolt is distinct amid the cloud fill.

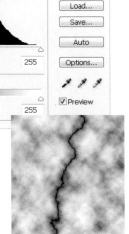

4 We want the lightning bolt to be white, with the surrounding area black, so go to **Image > Adjustments > Invert** (Ctrl/Cmd+I).

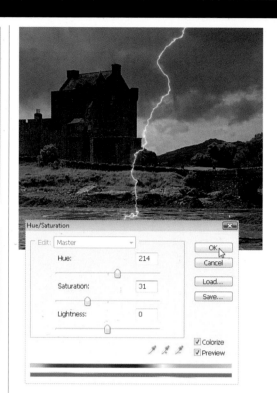

5 Again, choose **Image > Adjustments > Levels**. Grab the central gray point marker and drag it to the right until most of the clouds surrounding the lightning bolt have disappeared. Stop dragging the slider when just a few cloudy wisps remain attached to the bolt itself.

6 Now, set the blending mode for the Lightning layer to Screen to hide all of the black on the layer, leaving just the lightning visible. To color the lightning, go to **Image > Adjustments > Hue and Saturation**. Check the Colorize box and drag the Hue slider to the right until the lightning bolt is an electric blue color. Increase the Saturation value according to taste.

7 Choose the Rectangular Marquee tool and drag a selection around the unwanted lower half of the lightning bolt. Right-click/ Ctrl+click within the selection, and choose Layer Via Cut. This will paste this section onto a new layer.

8 Go to **Edit > Transform > Distort** to move the second branch of lightning into position at the top of the first bolt. Click and drag within the bounding box to move it. Click and drag the corner handles to distort the layer a little, altering the shape of the bolt.

95

Tip

TREMENDOUS TRANSFORMATIONS

In this project, we've made use of a transformation in Photoshop to position and distort the second bolt of lightning. These commands are useful for making adjustments to the size and shape of any element on a layer. Once in Transform mode (in this case Edit > Transform > Distort), you can adjust the size and shape of a layer element by dragging any of the handles attached to the surrounding bounding box. You can move a layer element while in Transform by simply placing your pointer within the box and dragging. There are a number of Transformations available: Distort, Rotate, Scale, Skew, and Perspective. When you have made your adjustments to the layer, click the Commit checkmark in the Options bar to apply the changes, or simply double-click within the bounding box.

Creating snow

Here we'll take a distinctly un-winter-like shot and dress it in a blanket of snow, adding quite a blizzard to boot. For a relatively simple technique, the end result is surprisingly sophisticated and effective. To generate the first covering of snow we'll make a simple selection via the Color Range selection command. For the falling snow we'll use the Noise filter, modifying this so the snowflakes clump together. Of course, snow is at its most picturesque when it's being blown around by a chill winter wind, and we can use the Motion Blur filter here.

So, get wrapped up and ready to create a winter wonderland, courtesy of Photoshop!

1 First, we need to begin with this distinctly summertime image and generate a layer of snow to cover the ground and trees. Choose the Eyedropper tool from the Toolbar and click in the field to sample a mid-range green color. We now need to make a selection based on the distribution of this colour throughout the image. Go to **Select** > **Color Range**. Use a Fuzziness slider setting of 132 and choose Sampled Color from the Select box. Click OK.

2 Add a new layer, naming it "Snow." We need to fill this active selection with white to begin the snow effect, so go to **Edit** > **Fill**, and choose White for Contents.

3 The image needs to be made a little colder now. Add another layer and click in the foreground color swatch, choosing a vibrant blue/violet. Select the Gradient tool from the Toolbar and click in the Gradient Picker, choosing Foreground To Transparent. Click and hold with the tool at the bottom of the image and drag the gradient guide vertically to the top. Set the blending mode for this layer to Hue and the layer opacity to 80%.

4 Now to add some snow. Add another new layer (Ctrl+Shift+N) and name it "Snowfall." Fill this layer with 50% Gray via **Edit** > **Fill** > **Contents: 50% Gray**. To begin creating the snowfall, we need to add some noise to this layer. Hit D to revert to default Black/White colors, and go to **Filter** > **Noise** > **Add Noise**.

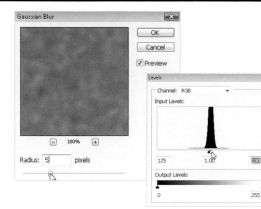

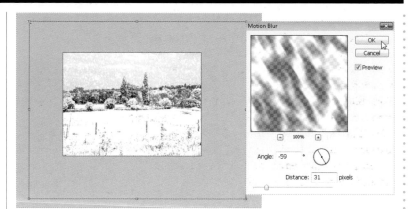

5 In the Add Noise dialog, drag the Amount slider up to 50%. Choose Gaussian for Distribution and check the Monochrome checkbox. Click OK. This noise is too fine for a snow effect, so blur this layer with **Filter > Blur > Gaussian Blur**. Use a Blur Radius of 5 pixels to clump the noise a little.

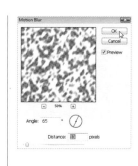

7 Set the blending mode for this layer to Screen to allow the landscape to show through the snow. To blur the snow and give it some movement, first go to **Filter > Convert For Smart Filters**. Now, go to **Filter > Blur > Motion Blur**. Use an Angle of 65 degrees and a Distance of 13.

8 We need a few bigger snowflakes to give the impression of distance. Duplicate this Snow layer (Ctrl+J) and go to **Edit > Transform > Flip Horizontal**. Zoom out from the image using the Zoom tool and go to **Image > Transform > Scale**. We'll now make the snowflakes on this layer

bigger. Lock the chain-link in the Options bar to constrain the proportions, then drag the corner handle on the bounding box outwards. Hit the Enter key to commit the transformation.

9 Finally, on this duplicated snowfall layer, double-click the entry for the Motion Blur Smart Filter in the Layers palette. We want to blow this snow in the other direction, so use an Angle of −59 and a distance of 31.

6 We need to adjust the contrast of this layer, using **Image > Adjustments > Levels**. In the Levels dialog, select the white point marker and drag it to the left until it's below the center of the histogram peak. Now drag the Black Point marker to the right until it almost disappears behind the white marker. Click OK.

97

Tip

SMART SNOW!
Because we've used Smart Filters here to introduce some movement into the falling snow, you can re-adjust this at any time after you've applied the Motion Blur Smart Filter, simply by double-clicking the entry for it in the Layers palette. The Motion Blur filter dialog will open again, and you can change the angle and even the blur amount before clicking OK to apply the changes.

Adding reflections

Reflections are essentially mirror images of objects, but creating them accurately in Photoshop takes careful manipulation. In this example, we're going to look at how we can transform simple still-life subjects by adding realistic reflections.

We'll be controlling the opacity of the reflection by using a gradient applied to a layer mask. For an even more convincing effect, we'll also use a very subtle shadow to indicate a surface plane.

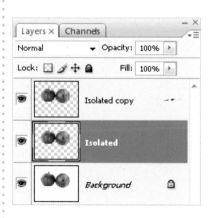

1 Here we'll create a realistic reflection from the two objects in this image. We want to create the illusion of the objects standing on a highly polished glass-like surface. First, we need to isolate the objects from the background. Select the Magic Wand tool from the Toolbar.

2 Set the Tolerance for the wand to 30 in the Options bar. Check the Anti-aliased and Contiguous boxes to ensure a smooth-edged, continuous selection. Now, click with the Wand anywhere in the white area that surrounds the objects. Go to **Select > Inverse** (Ctrl/Cmd+Shift+I) so that the apples are selected rather than the background.

3 Go to **Edit > Copy** (Ctrl/Cmd+C), and then to **Edit > Paste** (Ctrl/Cmd+V) to paste a copy of the selected objects onto another layer. Duplicate this new layer by going to **Layer > Duplicate Layer**.

4 We need to extend the canvas downward so we have some space for the shadows. Hit D on the keyboard to set white as the background color. Now go to **Image > Canvas Size**. Click in the top center square in the Anchor box, select Percent, enter 20 in the Height box, and choose Background for Canvas extension color. Click OK to extend the canvas downward.

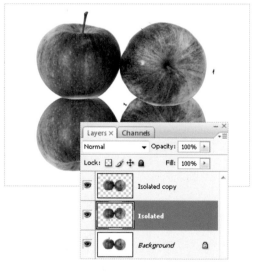

5 Now click on the lower Reflection layer in the Layers palette. We need to flip this layer vertically to begin creating the reflection, so do this using **Edit > Transform > Flip Vertical**. Hit M on the keyboard to activate the Move tool and then use the downward arrow key on the keyboard to move the reflection down the canvas. Moving the layer with the arrow keys will ensure that the reflection stays perfectly aligned with the actual apples. Don't forget that the two apple layers need to overlap a little. Using the Crop tool, crop away any large areas of white beneath the reflected apples.

Tip

ANOTHER SURFACE

As an attractive alternative, you can create the reflections so that they appear to be reflected in frosted glass rather than a perfectly smooth surface. When you've completed all of the steps, return to the Reflection layer and go to Filter > Distort > Glass. Choose Frosted for texture and adjust the size and the slider according to taste.

6 Still working on the Reflection layer, add a Layer Mask using **Layer > Layer Mask > Reveal All**. Now add a gradient to the mask to gradually dissolve the reflection. Choose the Gradient tool and click in the Gradient Picker. Check that the foreground color is black and choose the Foreground to Transparent gradient. Click OK.

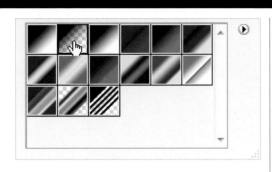

7 Click and drag with the Gradient tool from the very bottom of the image up to the top of the reflected apples. By holding down the Shift key while clicking and dragging, we can ensure that the gradient is perfectly horizontal. Once the gradient mask has completed, right-click/Ctrl+click the thumbnail for the mask in the Layers palette and choose Apply Mask.

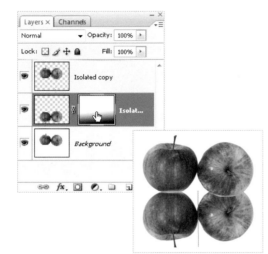

8 To add a little more realism, blur the Isolated layer using **Filter > Blur > Motion Blur**. Choose an Angle value of 90 degrees and 21 pixels for Distance. This will give a subtle effect of the surface distorting the reflection. Click OK and reduce the opacity of this layer to 75%.

9 Duplicate the Isolated copy layer (Ctrl/Cmd+J). Ctrl/Cmd-click the thumbnail for this layer to generate a selection from it. Choose a dark brown color for foreground and fill the selection using **Edit > Fill > Contents: Foreground Color**. Hit Ctrl/Cmd+D to deselect.

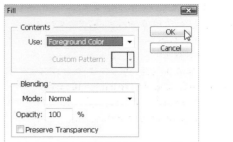

10 We need to make the shadows lie flat, so go to **Edit > Free Transform**. Grab the top center handle on the Transform bounding box, hold down the Ctrl/Cmd key, and drag it to the right to compress the shadows. Double-click within the bounding box to apply the Transform. In the Layers palette, drag this shadow layer down the stack so that it sits below the Isolated copy layer. Blur the shadow with **Filter > Blur > Gaussian Blur**, using a value of 34 pixels. Now reduce the opacity of this layer to 65%. Finally, use the Eraser tool at low opacity to partially erase the furthest points of the shadows.

Simulating sunsets

Sunsets are beautiful, but transient—and often somewhat elusive. Good sunsets can be caught on camera, but the odds are that they won't quite capture the majesty of the real thing.

Sometimes the result appears flat, and lacking in the russets, oranges, and warm gold tones provided by the setting sun. The good news is that, armed with Photoshop, we can simulate the evening sky's crowning glory very well indeed.

With the powerful Gradient tool, some well-chosen filters, and a little imagination, we have all the tools we need to turn day into brilliant dusk.

1 Begin the sunset conversion by adding a gradient on a separate layer. Open the original image, add a new layer (Ctrl/Cmd+Shift+N), and call it "Sunset." This image has a dull, but fairly cloudy, sky, so it's an ideal candidate. Click on the background color swatch and choose a bright yellow from the Color Picker. Now click the foreground swatch, and choose a bright orange/red.

3 Duplicate the original background layer (Ctrl/Cmd+J). Go to **Image > Adjustments > Photo Filter**. From the Photo Filter dialog box, choose Magenta from the Filter drop-down menu, and increase the Density slider to 84%. This will add a warm cast to the overall image.

2 Choose the Gradient tool and click in the Gradient Picker, selecting Foreground to Background. Select Linear Gradient from the Options bar. Click and drag with the tool from the very top of the image, releasing the mouse button on the horizon line. Set this layer to Linear Burn, reducing the opacity to 80%.

4 Now we need to add the sun. Click on the Sunset layer and select the Elliptical Marquee tool from the Toolbar. The tool is nested below the Rectangular Marquee tool, so click and hold on this tool to reveal it. Select Fixed Aspect Ratio from the Style box in the Options bar. Create a new layer (Ctrl/Cmd+Shift+N) at the top of the Layer stack called "Sun," and drag a small circle, overlapping the horizon.

Tip

IMAGE > ADJUSTMENTS > PHOTO FILTERS
The Photo Filters command in Photoshop CS3, as used here in step 3, is a great way to simulate traditional photographic filters, or to add a subtle color cast to an image. There is a huge range of different color filters to choose from, each selected using the Filter drop-down menu. The intensity of the color overlay is controlled with the Density slider, and checking Preserve Luminosity ensures that the image's original brightness and contrast level are not altered by the filter itself.

5 Choose a very light yellow for the foreground color and fill the selection by clicking in it with the Paint Bucket tool. Hit Ctrl/Cmd+D to deselect. Blur the sun a little with **Filter > Blur > Gaussian Blur**, using a Radius of 5.8. Set the blending mode for this layer to Vivid Light and reduce the opacity to 85%.

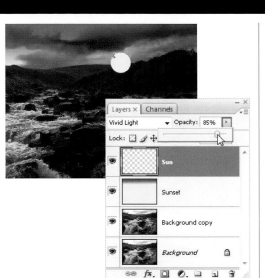

6 Remain on the Sun layer and choose the Brush tool from the Toolbar. Select a soft-edged brush from the Brush Picker, and reduce the Brush Opacity to 33% in the Options bar. Also in the Options bar, click on the Airbrush symbol. Now paint with bright yellow above the sun and between the clouds.

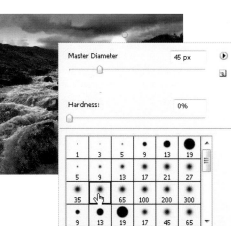

7 Now choose a very bright and vivid red. Paint with this color at low opacity along the very edge of the horizon line. Also paint with this color here and there in the water to give the effect of the reflected sky.

8 With the Eyedropper tool, sample the mauve color from the clouds. Paint some of this color at very low opacity over the top surfaces of some of the rocks, to reflect some color from the sky.

9 For the finishing touch, add a lens flare. Create a new layer at the top of the stack (Ctrl/Cmd+ Shift+N). Fill this layer with black using **Edit > Fill > Contents Use: Black**. Now go to **Filter > Render > Lens Flare**. Once the dialog box opens, choose 50-300 Zoom at a Brightness of 77%. Drag the crosshair for the lens flare up toward the top right. Hit OK. To hide the black, set the blending mode to Screen. Reduce the opacity to 79% and move the flare into position with the Move tool. Position the brightest flare directly

over the sun. Finally, select the Sunset layer and, with the Eraser tool, erase some of the yellow from the sunset layer to reveal the cooler magenta underneath. Use a large-sized brush and concentrate on the foreground area.

Day into night

Nighttime shots with a camera can be difficult at the best of times. With such low light levels, long exposures are needed, and it can be a pretty hit and miss affair to gauge such exposures.

Using a straightforward daytime shot, it's possible in Photoshop to simulate an after dark image, complete with atmospheric street lighting. Here we'll begin by using the ubiquitous Lighting filter as a Smart Filter to set the scene, adding soft radiating light beams and subtle glows with Gradients. Because it's applied as a Smart Filter, you can always adjust the lighting again later in the project. It's vitally important to remember that when it comes to artificial light sources, as we have here, the actual color of each light can vary to an enormous extent. By carefully controlling the hue and intensity of the added lights a wonderful degree of realism can be achieved.

So, fire up Photoshop and let dusk descend!

1 Open the original daytime image and duplicate the Background Layer (Ctrl-J), renaming it Night Layer. To set the scene, go to **Image > Adjustments > Hue/Saturation**. In the Hue/Sat dialog, check the Colorize box and also ensure Preview is checked so that you can see the changes. Now, move the Hue slider to 232, and the Saturation to 42. Darken the whole image by setting the Lightness to –90.

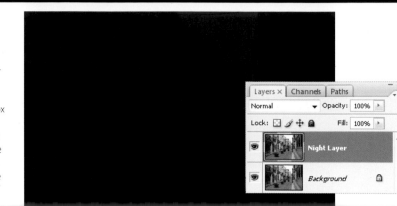

2 Now we'll introduce another color to liven things up a bit. Add a new layer (Ctrl-Shift-N) and choose the Gradient tool. Choose a deep petrol blue for the foreground color and click in the Gradient Picker, choosing Foreground to Transparent. Now, drag a gradient from the bottom left corner diagonally across the image. Set the blending mode for this layer to Hue.

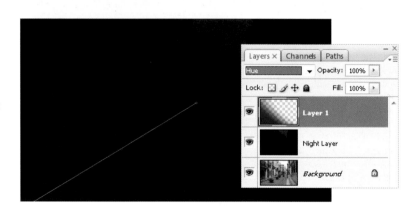

3 Click again on the Night layer and duplicate it (Ctrl-J). Now go to **Filter > Convert For Smart Filters**. Go to **Filter > Render > Lighting Effects**. Choose Blue Omni from the style box and Spotlight for Light Type. Drag the handles around the light pool in the preview box to position it as shown in the screenshot. Set the Intensity slider to 60 and click in the Light Color swatch, choosing a very light blue. Click OK. Set this layer to Lighten, Opacity 30%. You can always double-click this Smart Filter entry to adjust the lighting later.

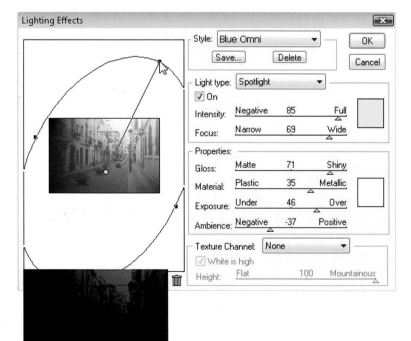

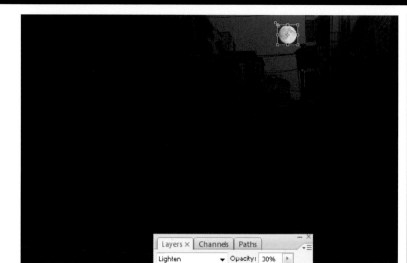

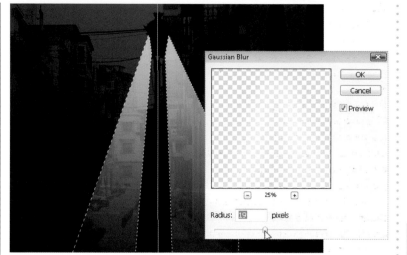

4 Open the moon image and go to **Select > All, Edit > Copy**. Then close the moon image and return to the main composition, choosing **Edit > Paste**. Size and position the moon via **Edit > Transform > Scale**. Hold down the Shift key while reducing the size of the moon with one of the corner handles. Set this layer to Screen blending mode.

6 Choose a bright yellow from the color palette and select the Gradient tool. Choose Radial Gradient from the Options bar. Click and drag the gradient from the top to the bottom of the street light. Hit Ctrl-D to deselect and set the layer blending mode to Screen. Blur via **Filter > Blur > Gaussian Blur**, using a Radius of 19 pixels.

5 To turn on the street lamps, add a new layer and choose the Polygon Lasso tool. Ensure that Add To Selection is active in the Options bar. Draw two selections from the nearesr lamp, radiating down to the ground. Go to **Select > Refine Edge** and use a Feather radius of 10 pixels.

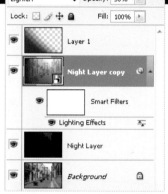

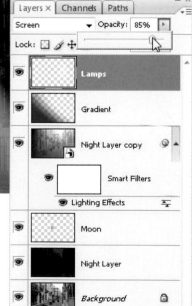

7 Add another new layer and zoom into the top of the lamp. With the Gradient tool, drag a very small gradient in the center of the lamp. Again, blur a little with Gaussian Blur and set the blending mode to Screen.

DAY INTO NIGHT

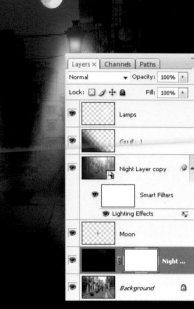

8 Now, duplicate these lamp light layers (by dragging them to the New Layer icon), and move the duplicated light beams into position on the other streelights in the image with the Move tool. You can size the light beams to fit the other lamps, using **Edit** > **Transform** > **Scale**.

9 Draw another large triangular selection over the first lamp, using the Polygon Lasso tool. Add another new layer and drag another gradient over this selection. Deselect and blur the layer, using **Filter** > **Blur** > **Gaussian Blur**, with a radius of 90. Set the blending mode to Screen. Duplicate this layer twice, placing the duplicates over the other lamps.

10 Return to the original Night layer and add a Layer Mask via **Layer** > **Add Layer Mask** > **Reveal All**. Select the Brush tool and choose a soft brush from the Picker. Now, paint with black at very low opacity around and beneath the streetlamps, to reveal a little color from the underlying Background layer. This will give the impression of the light illuminating the nearby building and ground.

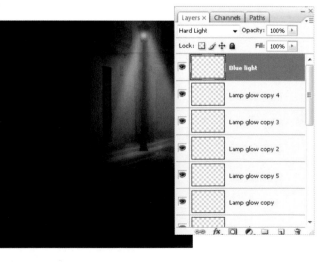

11 On a new layer, change the foreground colour to a vivid blue. With the Gradient Tool, drag a tiny gradient just in the doorway on the left to create a small light. Now on a separate layer, choose the Brush Tool. Using the brush at a large size, paint some reflected blue onto the pavement and the walls at very low opacity. Set this layer to Hard Light.

12 As a final touch, we need to add some lights to the car. Zoom right in to the car in the distance and choose the Polygon Lasso tool. Draw a selection for the headlight beam and choose a very light blue for foreground. With the Gradient tool, drag a gradient over the selection. Again, blur this a little, using Gaussian Blur. Set the layer blending mode to Screen.

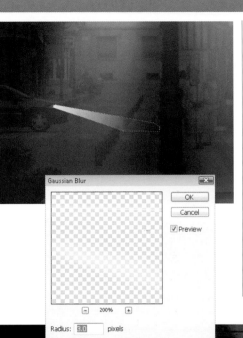

13 To finish off, use the Brush tool and a soft brush to add the red rear light on the car and various yellow orange lights in the distant windows of the buildings.

How many distant lights to add is really a matter of personal choice. A few stars can be also added to the night sky with a small brush.

TRADITIONAL PHOTOGRAPHIC EFFECTS

Vintage Hollywood portrait

Sabattier and solarization effect

Adding film grain

Infrared photography effect

Cross-processing effect

Hand tinting

Duotones

Vintage Hollywood portrait

Some of the most iconic portraits were black-and-white pictures of film stars, produced as publicity shots by the great Hollywood studios of the 1930s and 40s. The combination of dramatic lighting, a sumptuous tonal range, and flattering soft focus produced portraits that summed up the golden age of the silver screen.

As we'll demonstrate here, you don't need expensive studio setups to recreate such portrait shots, thanks to the power of Photoshop CS3 and its new Black & White command. Layer blending modes inject a bit of much-needed tonal punch, and we can manipulate the tones with the Dodge and Burn tools.

So, if you've always dreamed of Hollywood stardom, follow this recipe to create your own classic Hollywood portrait!

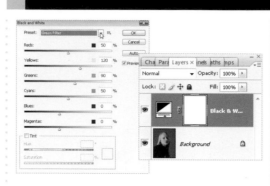

1 Open the start image and go to **Layer > New Adjustment Layer > Black & White**. In the Black & White dialog, choose Green Filter from the Presets. Click OK to apply the adjustment.

2 Click on the Background layer and duplicate it via **Layer > Duplicate Layer**. Set the blending mode for this layer to Overlay, and set the opacity to around 45%. Go to **Layer > Flatten Image**.

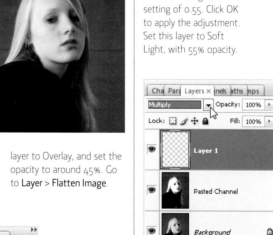

3 Click the Blue channel in the Channels palette and go to **Select > All**. Copy the Blue channel using **Edit > Copy** (Ctrl/Cmd+V) and click on the RGB channel. Return to the Layers palette and **Edit > Paste** (Ctrl/Cmd+V) to paste the copied channel onto a separate layer.

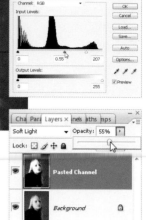

4 We need to adjust the contrast of this layer, so go to **Image > Adjustments > Levels**. Grab the White Point slider and drag it to the left, to a value of 207. Drag the Mid-point slider to the right, to a setting of 0.55. Click OK to apply the adjustment. Set this layer to Soft Light, with 55% opacity.

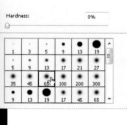

5 Add a new layer and set its blending mode to Multiply. Choose black as your foreground color and choose the Brush tool. From the Brush Picker, choose a soft, round brush. Set the brush opacity to 50%. Paint over the unwanted background around the head with this brush at a large size.

108

6 Use the brush at a much smaller size to paint under the chin and the nose, and within the eye sockets to darken them. When you're done, click on the Pasted Channel layer beneath this shading layer and go to **Layer > Merge Down**.

7 Duplicate the Background Layer (Ctrl/Cmd+J). Rename this layer "Dodge and Burn." Choose the Burn tool from the Toolbar and, in the Options bar, set Range to Midtones and Exposure to 6%. Choose a soft brush from the Brush Picker. Using this tool, begin to work over the underside of the nose, the lips, and within the upper areas of the eye sockets to gently darken these areas. Remember, we're trying to give the impression of a very harsh light falling from above. You can also use this tool at a very small size to darken the eyebrows.

8 Change the Range to Highlights and work over these areas a little more to darken any remaining highlight areas.

9 Change to the Dodge tool and set the Range to Highlights in the Options bar. Reduce the exposure to 2%. Use this tool over the highlights in the hair to lighten them. Using the brush at a very small size, and still with Highlights selected for Range, use this tool over the reflected light in the eyes and the highlights on the lips to lighten these areas, too.

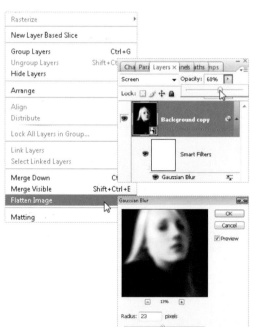

10 When you're happy with the shadows and highlights in the image, go to **Layer > Flatten Image**. Once flattened, duplicate the Background Layer. We're going to add some subtle soft focus to the image, so, on the duplicate layer, go to **Filter > Convert For Smart Filters**. Now go to **Filter > Blur > Gaussian Blur**. Use a blur radius of 23 pixels. Click OK. Set the layer blending mode to Screen and the opacity to 60%.

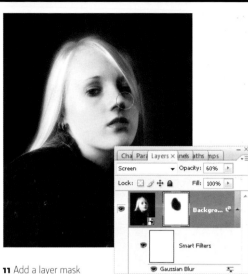

11 Add a layer mask using **Layer > Layer Mask > Reveal All**. Choose the Brush tool and, with a soft, round brush, paint over the central features of the face with black to hide the blur.

Sabattier and solarization effect

In the world of digital imaging, it's easy to lose sight of the fact that special effects existed long before the advent of computers and Photoshop. In the days of the traditional darkroom, there were many ways of manipulating the look and atmosphere of an image, and one of the most famous—the Sabattier effect—can still yield wonderfully magnetic and arresting images today when we recreate the effect in Photoshop.

Traditionally, the effect was achieved by exposing a partially developed print to light, where the normal tones and colors are reversed. In the darkroom, this was a hit-and-miss affair, but in Photoshop we have much more control.

The technique revolves primarily around the Curves command, where we can target specific tonal ranges.

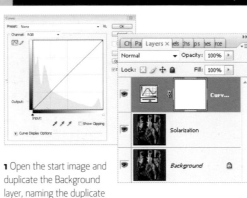

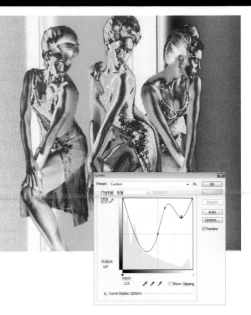

1 Open the start image and duplicate the Background layer, naming the duplicate "Solarization." We'll use Curves to create the Sabattier effect, but via an adjustment layer for more flexibility. So, go to **Layer > New**

Adjustment Layer > Curves. Click OK to the first dialog and the Curves dialog will be displayed. From the Channels option, select RGB.

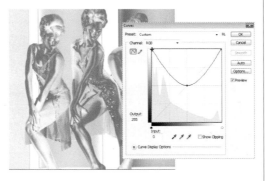

2 Start by clicking a point along the curve at the center of the grid. Grab the shadow point of the curve on the bottom left, and drag it to the top. This inverts all of the tones in the left-hand section of the tonal range, but leaves the values to the right of the center point virtually unchanged.

4 Now, click another point between this point and the white point at the top left of the curve. Drag this point down to the first grid line.

This curve shape gives a result similar to the previous one, but with a saturation boost for an even more psychedelic effect.

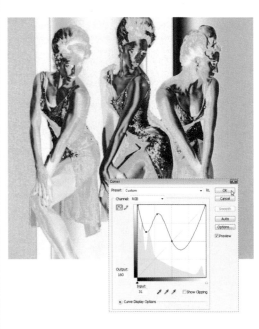

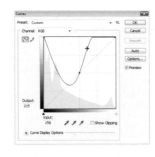

3 We're not concentrating on just basic solarization effects here, but looking at the variations we can create, starting from the basic technique. So, click another point on the curve a little way to the right of the center point. Drag this point up, as shown in the screenshot.

5 The curve shown here is virtually the opposite of the previous one, with the second dip within the shadow half of the curve. Remember, because we're using an adjustment layer, you can OK the dialog for each variation and simply double-click the adjustment layer to manipulate the curve for the next one.

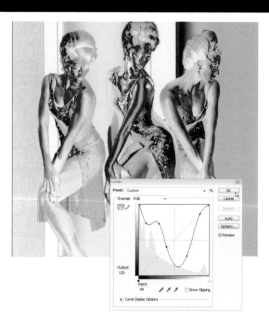

6 Don't be afraid to play with the curve a little, maintaining roughly the same basic shape. Here, we've used five points on the curve to create a more complicated variation, which creates a really dramatic, "Pop Art" effect.

7 To give yourself more creative scope, you can combine a number of these steps. Simply go to **Layer > Merge Down** after your first Curves adjustment, so you have the first solarization effect as a layer. Duplicate the Background layer and drag it to the top of the stack. Add a new Curves adjustment layer for the next effect and again go to **Layer > Merge Down**.

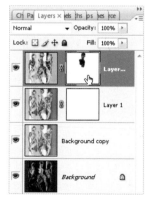

8 With all your merged solarization layers in place, add a layer mask to the upper layers via **Layer > Layer Mask > Reveal All**. Using a hard brush, with black as your foreground color, paint directly onto the layer masks to hide certain areas of each layer.

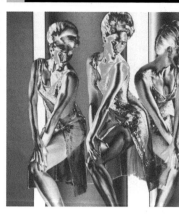

1 Solarization also works well in monochrome. To try this, use curves similar to those used in the color examples, then go to **Image > Adjustments > Desaturate** on the Solarization layer.

2 Black-and-white solarization examples often need a Levels adjustment to add the required amount of tonal impact. Once you've set your curve, go to **Layer > New Adjustment Layer > Levels**. Grab the Shadow point and drag it to the right, settling it beneath the very start of the histogram.

111

Tip

SAVING CURVES

Often you'll find that a particular curve creates a really good Sabattier effect, and it can be quite tricky to replicate the exact shape of the curve at a later date. It's a good idea to save the curve so you can easily load it again in future. To save a curve, hit the small Preset Options icon at the top of the Curves dialog, choosing Save Preset. Give your curve a name and save it to a suitable location. You can load a saved curve via the same Preset Options button.

Adding film grain

In traditional film photography, films of a faster speed, or higher light sensitivity, produce visible "grain" within the final printed image. Although this is often viewed as a shortcoming of fast films, it is also something which can be deliberately exploited with some truly artistic results. It's true that digital cameras, used at a higher ISO setting, produce their own kind of grain, something known as noise. However, in-camera, we have very little control over this phenomenon, and digital noise created with the camera is not as pleasing an effect as the careful exploitation of film grain. Adding the effect of film grain after the event and applying it to a near noiseless image gives us a far greater degree of control over the effect.

Grain in color images

1 It's important to apply the Film Grain filter on a duplicate layer, so that layer blending modes can be used to modify the effect. Duplicate the original Background layer by dragging it to the "Create a new layer" icon at the base of the Layers palette (or hit Ctrl/Cmd+J).

2 The Film Grain filter works best on a grayscale layer, so go to **Image > Adjustments > Desaturate**. To experiment with the grain, we're going to use a Smart Filter, so, on the desaturated layer, go to **Filter > Convert For Smart Filters**. To add grain, go to **Filter > Artistic > Film Grain**. Set the Grain slider to 20, Highlight Area 11, Intensity 2. Click OK.

3 On the grain layer, change the blending mode to Overlay. You can reduce the effect if necessary by reducing the opacity of this layer. To make the grain a bit more realistic, go to **Filter > Noise > Median** and use a radius value of 2 pixels. This will blur the grain a little, making the effect more natural and less mechanical.

4 A more subtle effect can be created by using a Hard Light blending mode for the grain layer and adjusting its opacity. Both methods give excellent results.

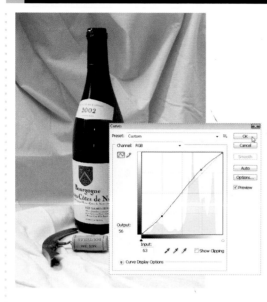

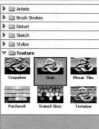

1 Film Grain works especially well on monochrome images. Begin by desaturating the Background layer of your chosen image via **Image > Adjustments > Desaturate**. For a dramatic effect, increase the contrast by using Curves (**Image > Adjustments > Curves**). Replicate the curve shown in the screenshot; it is the classic curve for a subtle increase in contrast.

3 An alternative to the Film Grain filter is the Grain filter, which can be found under **Filter > Texture > Grain**. The essential difference here is that you can select a variety of distribution patterns for the grain. Access these via the Grain Type drop-down in the Filter dialog. For a really dramatic effect, try the Enlarged grain type.

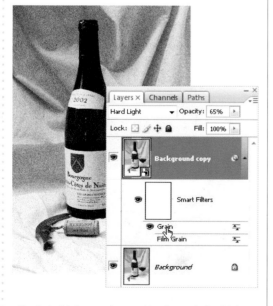

2 Duplicate this layer and again go to **Filter > Convert For Smart Filters**. Now return to **Filter > Artistic > Film Grain**, using the same settings as in Step 2. Set the blending mode for this layer to Hard Light. You can control the strength of the grain effect by reducing the opacity of the grain layer.

Contrasty

4 Remember, because we're applying the grain via a Smart Filter, you can choose another grain type by simply

Sprinkles

double-clicking the entry for the filter in the Layers palette and then choosing another grain variety from

Horizontal

within the filter itself. Some examples of the available grain types are shown above.

Speckle

113

Infrared photography effect

Traditionally, black-and-white infrared photography involves the use of special filters and film stock that is only sensitive to light which emanates from the far end of the visible spectrum of light. Many digital cameras are capable of "seeing" this essentially invisible light, but infrared photography is not just the preserve of those who posses the correct filters and techniques; it's something that can be replicated from full color digital images in Photoshop. Essentially, an infrared photograph gains its mysterious and otherworldly qualities from the infrared light being reflected back into the camera at different strengths, depending on the local color of elements within the subject. Some local colors reflect a lot of infrared light, so trees and foliage take on an ethereal white glow, skin tones adopt a rather waxy, ghost-like quality, and blue summer skies are rendered almost black. To add to the mix, the whole image adopts a soft, glowing quality for truly unique, monochrome images.

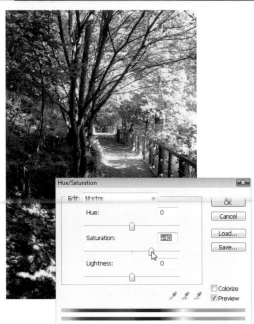

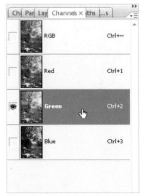

1 Images that contain lots of green foliage are ideally suited to this technique. Open your start image and increase the saturation a little using **Image** > **Adjustments** > **Hue and Saturation**. Drag the Saturation slider to the right until the foliage is quite vivid. Here I've used a value of +40.

2 We'll apply the infrared effect to a duplicate layer. Hit Ctrl/Cmd+D to duplicate the Background layer. Now, click on the Channels palette tab and select the Green channel.

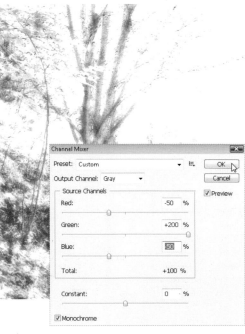

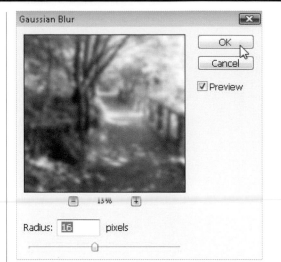

3 To create the infrared glow, we need to blur this channel. Go to **Filter** > **Blur** > **Gaussian Blur** and use a radius of 16 pixels. Click back on the RGB channel and return to the Layers palette, choosing the duplicate layer. Set the blending mode for this layer to Screen.

4 This layer needs to be monochrome, and we need to adjust the channel ratios. Add a Channel Mixer adjustment layer using **Layer** > **New Adjustment Layer** > **Channel Mixer**. First we need to intensify the Green channel, so drag the slider for the channel to +200. Set the Red slider to −50 and the Blue slider to −50. Click the Monochrome checkbox.

Tip

THREE WAYS TO DUPLICATE A LAYER

In many of the recipes in this book, we start by making a duplicate copy of a layer.

There are three ways to do this—choose whichever method suits you best:

1 Drag the layer to the "Create a new layer" icon at the base of the Layers palette.
2 Use the Layers menu; choose Layer > Duplicate Layer.
3 Use a keyboard shortcut. Simply hold down the Ctrl/Cmd key and hit J.

5 Now we're really getting to that Infrared like ghostly effect, but the opacity of the infrared layer needs reducing for a better effect. Click on the layer and reduce the opacity to 32%.

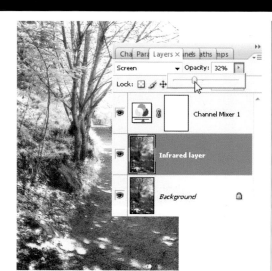

8 As a final touch, flatten the image, using **Layer > Flatten Image**, then go to **Image > Adjustments > Curves**. Drag the curve to create a subtle "S" shape to increase the contrast a little.

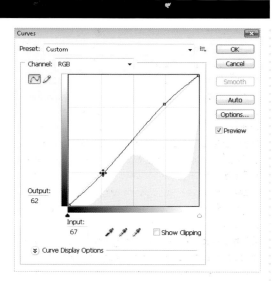

6 Infrared images are normally very grainy due to the qualities of the film stock used, although at the same time the image retains a high degree of detail. To replicate this we need to add some noise to the background layer. Click on this layer and go to **Filter > Noise > Add Noise**. Drag the Amount slider to 20%, select Uniform for Distribution, and ensure that Monochrome is checked. For a higher level of noise, simply increase the Amount value, although a higher value tends to flatten the tones in the image.

7 To control the overall intensity of the infrared effect, simply increase or decrease the opacity of the middle layer. Here I've increased the opacity to 53% for more impact.

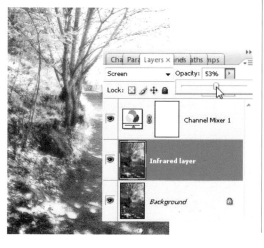

115

Cross-processing effect

Back in the days of wet-process photography, there were specific chemical processes for particular film types, and mix-and-match was not recommended by the manufacturers. However, since true creativity is often about breaking the rules, some photographers experimented with cross-processing, deliberately developing slide film with the chemicals meant for print film. The resulting images had a striking and distinctive look, and, while the process could be a bit unpredictable, when it worked, it worked well. The characteristics of the effect are over-saturated colors and an overall color shift, blown highlights, deep rich blacks, and marked contrast. In Photoshop we have more control over the effect, as we can tweak layers and experiment with individual color channels—with stunning results.

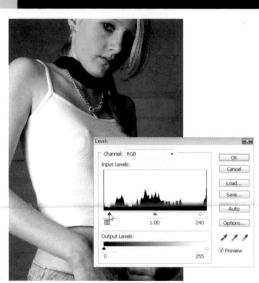

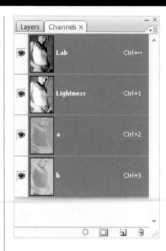

1 The cross-processing effect works best with high-contrast images with very saturated colors, so open the image and go to **Image > Adjustments > Levels**. Drag the White Point slider to the left and the Black Point to the right to pump up the contrast.

2 For the saturation boost, go to **Image > Adjustments > Hue/Saturation** and drag the Saturation slider to the right until the colors in the original image are quite vivid.

3 We need to change the color mode, and we'll do that on a duplicate file (**Image > Duplicate**). On the duplicate image, go to **Image > Mode > Lab Color**.

We'll be working on the individual Lab channels, so click on the Channels tab at the top of the Layers palette.

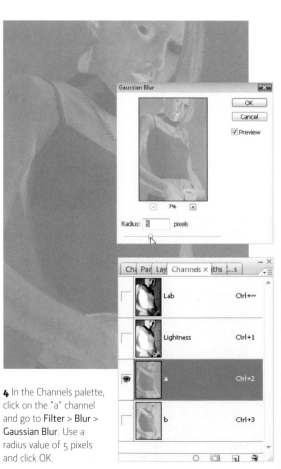

4 In the Channels palette, click on the "a" channel and go to **Filter > Blur > Gaussian Blur**. Use a radius value of 5 pixels and click OK.

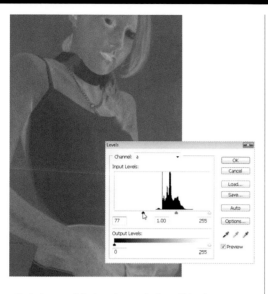

8 Working on the original image file, go to **Edit** > **Paste** (Ctrl/Cmd+V). Change the layer blending mode for this pasted layer to Overlay in the Layers palette to achieve the cross-processing effect.

5 Go to **Image** > **Adjustments** > **Levels** and drag the Black Point slider to the right until the Input Value box reads 77. Click OK.

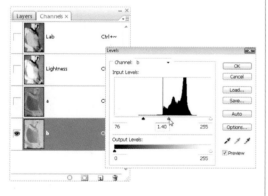

6 Now click on the "b" channel in the Channels palette. Go again to **Image** > **Adjustments** > **Levels**, drag the Black Point slider to the right until the Input Value box reads 76, and then enter 1.4 in the central (Gamma) box.

7 Click on the Lab channel and go to **Select** > **All** (Ctrl/Cmd+A), then **Edit** > **Copy** (Ctrl/Cmd+C) to copy the entire background layer with all channels intact. This duplicate image can now be closed without saving, and we can return to the original image.

9 To intensify the effect, duplicate this layer by right-clicking/Ctrl-clicking it in the Layers palette, and choosing Duplicate Layer. As a final touch, we can experiment with modifying the levels (**Image** > **Adjustment** > **Levels**) for either of these layers until a good result is reached.

Hand tinting

Before the age of color film, when black-and-white photography was the only option, it was common practice for photographers to tint a black-and-white image with colored dyes to mimic real-life colors. Although we now have all the advantages of stunning color photography, we can still use Photoshop to replicate this technique and add great charm to black-and-white images.

What we're looking for here is not truly lifelike color, but a decorative and subtle effect. Essentially, we can tint as little or as much of the image as we like, but the effect works best where areas of color are contrasted with the uncolored grayscale image.

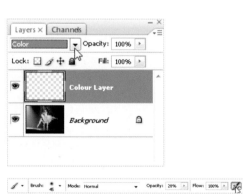

1 Open a suitable image and go to **Image > Mode**. If the original image is in color, first convert it to grayscale. Then convert it back to RGB so we can add color back into it. If the original is grayscale, it'll need to be converted to RGB mode.

3 Hit F6 on the keyboard to display the Colors palette. This is where we'll choose all of the painting colors. To choose a color, pass the mouse pointer over the spectrum bar and click to choose the approximate color. The colors can be fine-tuned with the RGB sliders above the bar, and the chosen color can be seen in the foreground swatch.

2 The color needs to be painted onto a separate layer, so create a new layer (Ctrl/Cmd+Shift+N). Set the blending mode for this layer to Color in the Layers palette. This mode will allow any added color to overlay the image. Now, choose the Brush tool and select a soft-edged brush from the Brush Picker. In the Options bar, set the brush opacity to 50% and activate the Airbrush icon.

4 Begin by choosing a warm yellow/orange. Paint over all of the areas of flesh with this color. Remember, because the brush is in Airbrush mode, the color will build up on the image if we leave it in one position for too long, so we need to keep it moving at all times. Vary the skin color slightly by occasionally dragging the RGB sliders. Remember, we only want to tint the image with color.

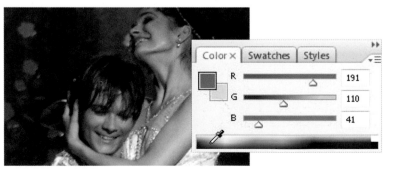

5 Now, choose a deep brown and paint over the hair of both dancers. Again, modify the color and tone using the sliders to introduce a little variety.

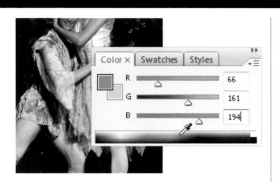

6 I've chosen a light blue to paint over the male dancer's costume. Essentially, we want less color over the lighter parts of the costume and heavier pigment over the darker parts. To make the accurate application of color easier, zoom into the image and adjust the size of the brush with the square bracket keys on the keyboard. Again, modify the color after applying the initial covering of blue and add a few touches of a darker purple shade.

8 Here, I've continued to paint yellows and oranges into the dancer's tutu using the Brush tool on the tinting layer.

9 To complete the image, I've zoomed into the ballerina's feet and applied a little color to her shoes.

Tip

MAKING A SELECTION WITH QUICK MASK
Quick Mask mode is a great way to make accurate selections. Enter Quick Mask by hitting Q on the keyboard. With black as the foreground color, paint an overlay onto the image over any areas of the image you wish to select. The masked areas will appear to be red, even though you are painting with black as the foreground color. When you have painted all of the areas you want to select, hit Q again to quit Quick Mask mode. You will now have an active selection in the shape of the mask you just painted.

119

7 To help keep the colors separate in complicated areas, try selecting a particular area first and then painting within the active selection. Here I've isolated the dancer's bodice by painting a Quick Mask onto the area first. (See the Tip box for more on using Quick Mask mode.) Exit Quick Mask mode (hit Q) to activate the selection, and paint the color into the selection.

Duotones

Basically, duotones are two-toned images (usually black and a second color). The use of the second color extends the tonal range of an image beyond that which is possible with just one color. In a duotone, you can map the distribution and density of the two colors across the tonal range of the image with pinpoint precision. The colors in duotones—with the exception of black—are known as "spot colors." These are industry-standard, predictable shades of ink used by printers to maintain consistent color in their print jobs.

In Photoshop, duotones can be created via the Duotone option in the Mode menu. (Monotones, Tritones, and Quadtones are also available, and are accessed from the Duotone dialog box.) If you're tired of straight black and white, just follow the steps in this recipe to add some color and depth to your images.

1 Open the original color image. Before the image can be converted to a duotone, we need to change the color image to grayscale, so go to **Image > Mode > Grayscale**. Answer OK to the "Discard Color Information" dialog box and save the grayscale image under a different filename.

3 Photoshop includes a variety of Duotone settings. To access them, click on the Load button. Choose the Process Duotones folder and select Magenta BL2 from the list. Click the Load button to confirm.

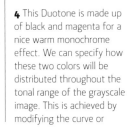

2 To begin the duotone process, go to **Image > Mode > Duotone**. In the Duotone options dialog box, choose Duotone from the Type box. This dialog box is "control central" when it comes to controlling the properties and appearance of the Duo/Tri/Quadtone. In the next few steps we'll concentrate on making adjustments to the properties here. Make sure that the Preview box is checked.

4 This Duotone is made up of black and magenta for a nice warm monochrome effect. We can specify how these two colors will be distributed throughout the tonal range of the grayscale image. This is achieved by modifying the curve or density ramp for each of the colors. It's generally best to leave the distribution of the black ink at the default, but we can modify the distribution of the magenta. Hit the Duotone Curve thumbnail for Ink 2.

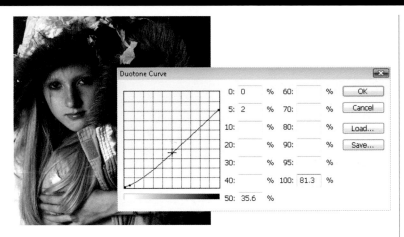

5 The distribution of the separate inks in Duotone mode is controlled using a curve or density ramp for each individual ink. These curves work in a way similar to conventional curves in Photoshop. The tonal range within the original grayscale image is represented by a graph with a curve straddling the entire tonal scale. Highlights are represented on the left side of the graph, the middle represents the midtones, and the darkest tones are on the right. The height of the curve at a particular tonal point in the graph designates the color density at that tone in the grayscale image. The various tones in the image are represented by percentage boxes to the right of the curve graph in 10% increments of tonality.

6 To increase the intensity of magenta in the midtone range, grab the handle near the center of the curve and drag it upward. Dragging a color's curve up will darken the color in the image, dragging it down will lighten it. When a suitable color density is achieved, click OK.

8 We're not limited to the supplied presets: we can choose alternate colors by simply clicking the ink swatches in the dialog box and choosing a color from the Picker. Here I've replaced the black ink with bright red, and chosen a vivid pink for my second ink.

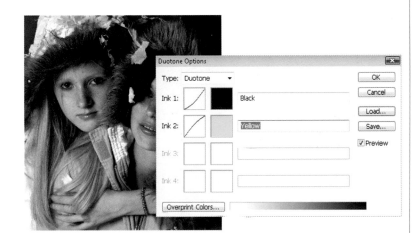

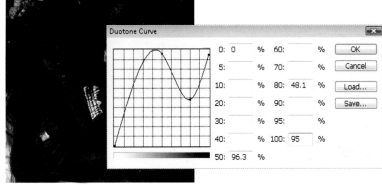

7 We can choose an alternative duotone combination at any time, simply by returning to **Image > Mode > Duotone.** Click the Load button again and choose a different Duotone preset. This Duotone preset uses black and yellow.

9 Although duotones are generally used to create subtly tinted images, when extreme adjustments are made to the ink curves some surprising and surreal effects can be achieved.

121

Tip

TRITONES AND QUADTONES

In a duotone, you use just two colors, or inks, to create the image. However, you can take the concept of duotones a couple of steps further with tritones and quadtones. As their names suggest, these siblings of the duotone process use three and four colors, respectively. Photoshop includes a large selection of preset tritone and quadtone combinations, which can be accessed from the main Duotone dialog box. Just choose Tritone or Quadtone from the Type box, and try some of the same techniques used in this example.

DISTORTION EFFECTS

Caricatures

The art of caricature dates back hundreds of years, and many celebrities are often more recognizable in a caricature than they are in a straightforward photograph. Caricature artists are extremely talented experts, with a keen eye and impeccable drawing ability. If you've ever wanted to create your own caricature, but have never felt you had the ability, Photoshop's got the answer.

In this recipe, we're going to take a simple portrait photograph and transform it into a caricature, using Photoshop's Transform command and the Liquify filter. This is a fun job, so why not sit back, fire up Photoshop, and caricature your boss? Trust me, you'll feel so much better!

1 Click on the Background layer and choose the Lasso tool. Set Feather to 10 pixels in the Options bar. Draw a rough selection around the nose, then right-click within the selection and choose Layer Via Copy. Label this layer "Nose."

2 Repeat the procedure above to make selections around the mouth and the chin, generating another Layer Via Copy for each.

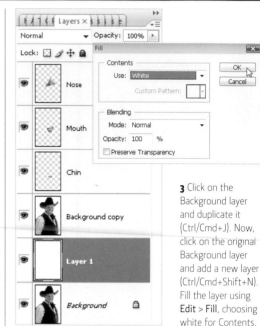

3 Click on the Background layer and duplicate it (Ctrl/Cmd+J). Now, click on the original Background layer and add a new layer (Ctrl/Cmd+Shift+N). Fill the layer using **Edit > Fill**, choosing white for Contents.

4 To begin the distortion, hide all of the feature layers by clicking the visibility eyes in the Layers palette, leaving just the Background Copy layer above the white fill visible. Click on the Background Copy and go to **Edit > Transform > Distort**. Drag the top corner handles on the distortion bounding box outwards. Grab the top middle handle and drag it upwards. Drag the bottom handles inwards a little to narrow the body and lower the face. Click the commit tick in the Options bar when you're done.

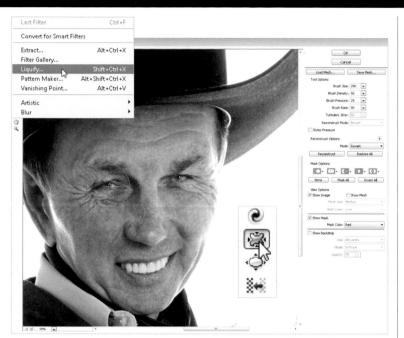

5 Go to **Filter** > **Liquify**. In the Liquify dialog, choose the Zoom tool and zoom into the eyes. Choose the Pucker tool from the

Toolbar. Using the right bracket key on the keyboard, increase the size of the brush so that it is as big as one of the eyes.

Using single clicks, click on the eyes to make them much smaller. Click OK to apply the Liquify result.

7 Add a layer mask by choosing **Layer** > **Layer Mask** > **Reveal All.** Choose the Brush tool and select a hard brush from the Brush Picker. Click directly on the layer mask and make sure that

your foreground color is black. Paint under the nose with this brush to hide the unwanted skin. Paint up to the lower outline of the nose. Click in the Brush Picker and reduce the

Hardness to 0%. Reduce the Brush opacity to 40%. Paint with black to erase the skin around the nose and blend it with the face.

6 Click on the Nose layer to make it visible again, using the visibility eye. Use the Move tool (V) to drag the nose roughly into position. Again, go to **Edit** > **Transform** > **Distort**. Drag the center side handles out and the bottom handle down to make the nose wider and longer. Drag the bottom corner handle out to widen the nose at the bottom. Position the nose by dragging within the bounding box.

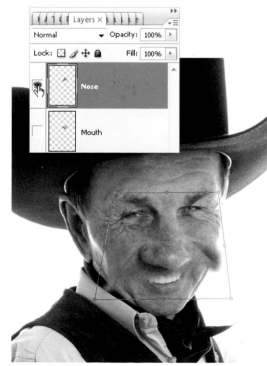

8 Click on the mouth layer and click its visibility eye to make it visible. Move the mouth into position, using the Move tool (V). Using **Edit** > **Transform** > **Scale**, increase the width and depth of the mouth by dragging on the handles around the bounding box. Hit Enter to commit.

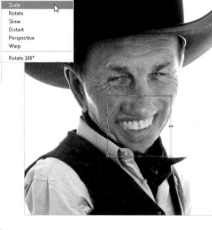

9 Select the Chin layer and return to **Edit** > **Transform** > **Distort**. Drag the handles into the shape shown in the screenshot to distort and point the chin. Make sure that the new chin fits with the sides of the face by carefully adjusting the handles.

Creating caricatures continued

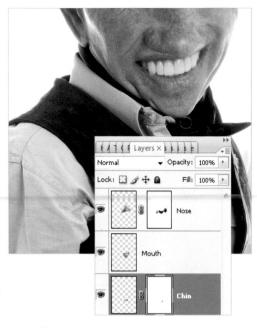

10 By adding a layer mask to each of the feature layers, you can paint on each mask with black to hide any unwanted areas and blend each feature in with the face beneath it.

11 Click on the top layer and repeatedly go to **Layer > Merge Down** until you have just one merged layer remaining above the white fill layer.

12 On your merged layer, return to **Filter > Liquify**. Choose the Forward Warp tool from the Toolbar. In the Tool Options, set the Brush Pressure to 20 and the Brush Size to around 200. Gently drag the cheekbones outwards on both sides of the face and push the eyebrows and corner of the mouth up a little.

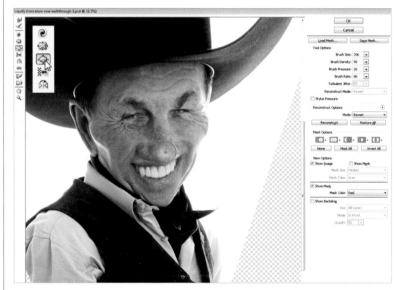

13 Choose the Bloat tool and increase the size of the brush so it is the same size as the end of the nose. Bloat the nose a little with just a few clicks.

14 At this stage you can do as much within the Liquify filter as you like, using the two tools above, gently pushing and pulling parts of the head. When you're happy with the result, click OK to apply the Liquify filter.

126

Smart Blur

Radius: 5.1

Threshold: 12.7

Quality: High

Mode: Normal

15 To give the image a more illustrative quality, go to **Filter > Blur > Smart Blur**. Use these settings: Radius 5.1, Threshold 12.7, Quality High.

17 Finally, flatten the image, using **Layer > Flatten Image**. Use the Crop tool to remove any empty areas around the outside of the image.

Arrange
Align
Distribute
Lock All Layers in Group...
Link Layers
Select Linked Layers
Merge Down   Ctrl+E
Merge Visible   Shift+Ctrl+E
Flatten Image
Matting

Glowing Edges (12.5%)

Artistic
Brush Strokes
Distort
Sketch
Stylize
Glowing Edges
Texture

OK
Cancel

Glowing Edges

Edge Width   3
Edge Brightness   20
Smoothness   14

Glowing Edges

Mode   ▶
Adjustments   ▶   Levels...   Ctrl+L
                                     Auto Levels   Shift+Ctrl+L
Duplicate...   Auto Contrast   Alt+Shift+Ctrl+L
Apply Image...   Auto Color   Shift+Ctrl+B
Calculations...   Curves...   Ctrl+M
                                     Color Balance...   Ctrl+B
Image Size...   Alt+Ctrl+I   Brightness/Contrast...
Canvas Size...   Alt+Ctrl+C   Black & White... Alt+Shift+Ctrl+B
Pixel Aspect Ratio   ▶   Hue/Saturation...   Ctrl+U
Rotate Canvas   ▶   Desaturate   Shift+Ctrl+U
Crop   Match Color...
Trim...   Replace Color...
Reveal All   Selective Color...
                                     Channel Mixer...
Variables   ▶   Gradient Map...
Apply Data Set...   Photo Filter...
                                     Shadow/Highlight...
                                     Exposure...

16 Duplicate again and go to **Filter > Stylize > Glowing Edges**. Use Edge Width 3, Edge Brightness 20 and Smoothness 14. Click OK, then go to **Image>Adjustments > Desaturate**, followed by **Image >**

Adjustments > Invert. Set the blending mode for this layer to Darken and reduce the opacity for a more subtle effect.

Layers

Darken   Opacity: 28%
Lock:

Background copy 3

Soft focus and selective depth of field

Soft focus is the classic way to create romantic portraits. In camera this is achieved by the use of special softening filters, but the same effect can be achieved very simply in Photoshop. Soft focus is not simply blurring an image, as we need to preserve the detail while adding an overlay of romantic softening that creates wonderful halos around highlights.

Selective focus, on the other hand, is a recipe we can use in Photoshop to recreate convincing depth-of-field effects, where there is an increasing fall-off of focus in front of and behind the main subject or focal point.

This wonderful pictorial device has great power when it comes to directing the viewer's attention. There are two ways of achieving this in Photoshop. We can simulate selective focus manually, with the Gaussian Blur filter and a layer mask, which can do a pretty good job. Alternatively, in Photoshop CS3, we have the new Lens Blur filter, which can simulate selective focus with stunning accuracy and realism. We'll be looking at both methods here.

Soft focus

1 Open the image and duplicate the background layer by dragging it to the "Create a new layer" icon in the Layers palette. Blur this duplicate layer, using **Filter > Blur > Gaussian Blur**. Use a Blur radius of anywhere between 30 and 50 pixels. The higher the setting, the more pronounced the effect will be in the final image. Here, I've used a value of 31.0 for a moderate blur.

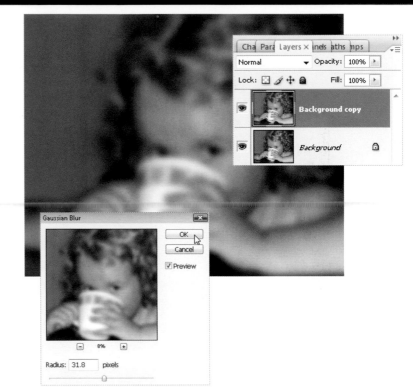

2 In the Layers palette, reduce the opacity of the blurred layer to allow some of the detail from the background to show through. The lower you set the opacity, the more subtle the soft focus effect will be. As a rule, you should use an opacity somewhere between 50% and 70%.

3 Choose the Eraser tool and select a soft brush from the Brush Picker. Reduce the Eraser opacity to 20% in the Options bar. Gently erase the blur over the eyes and the fingernails. At this opacity, the blur will not be entirely erased, but you will bring a little focus back into the features.

4 We need to add an extra glow to the highlights, so choose the Eyedropper tool and click in the lightest part of the hair to sample the color. Go to **Select** > **Color Range** and use a Fuzziness slider setting of 70. This will determine the range of colors selected. Choose Black Matte from the Selection Preview box so that we can see which parts will be selected.

5 With the selection active, add a new empty layer (Ctrl/Cmd+Shift+N). Fill the selected areas with white, using **Edit** > **Fill** > **Use: White**. Blur this highlight layer, using Gaussian Blur with with a high radius value of 100. Set the blending mode for this layer to Screen and reduce the opacity.

DISTORTION EFFECTS

Selective focus

1 For the first selective focus technique, we'll use the Gaussian Blur filter. First, duplicate the Background layer (Ctrl/Cmd+J). Go to **Filter > Blur > Gaussian Blur** and use a radius of 10, making sure that the Preview box is checked. We can make the depth-of-field effect more pronounced by using a higher value.

2 Add a layer mask, using **Layer > Layer Mask > Reveal All**. Ensure that you are working on the layer mask by checking for a bold outline around its thumbnail. Also make sure that the foreground color is black and the background color is white. Choose the Gradient tool and select Foreground to Background from the Gradient Picker. Choose Reflected Gradient from the Options bar.

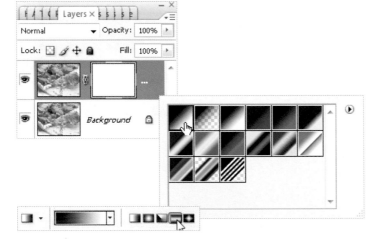

3 We want to create a very narrow area of focus, so click and drag with the Gradient tool vertically over the ring. The width of the gradient determines where the focus will fall off in the image. Note that the layer mask now has a fading black gradient across its center, allowing some of the underlying layer to show through the blur.

Selective focus with the Lens Blur filter

The previous method gives fairly good results, but now let's try the Lens Blur filter available in Photoshop CS3.

1 Starting with the original sharply focused image, we'll use an alpha channel to control the focus area for the Lens Blur filter. Begin by clicking on the tab for the Channels palette. Click on the "Create new channel" button at the base of the palette.

2 Next, choose the Gradient tool and set white as the foreground color and black as background. Hit the swap arrow next to the swatches if these are the wrong way around (or hit X on the keyboard). Click in the Gradient Picker and choose Foreground to Background. Choose Reflected Gradient from the Options bar.

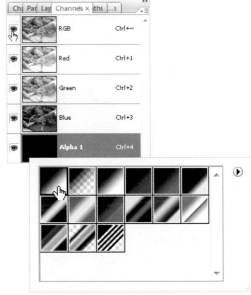

Tip

CHANGING CHANNELS

When using the Lens Blur filter, we use an alpha channel to describe the depth of field within the image. Normally, full color RGB images are made up of three channels: Red, Green, and Blue, simply described as RGB. When you add an additional channel, as you do here, this extra channel is known as an alpha channel. If you add just one extra channel, Photoshop will name it Alpha 1. When using the Lens Blur filter, we fill this alpha channel with a Black-to-White gradient. The filter interprets the white end of the gradient as in focus and the black end of the gradient as out of focus, and the areas between these two points are affected accordingly. You can access the Channels palette by clicking its tab (next to the Layers palette tab) or using Window > Channels.

130

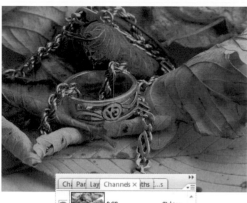

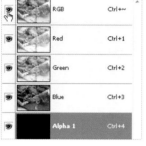

3 With the new alpha channel selected in the Channels palette, click the visibility eye next to the RGB channel at the top of the stack. The black fill will change to a red overlay as Photoshop enters Quick Mask mode. Starting near the bottom of the ring, click and drag upward with the Gradient tool, releasing the mouse button just above the top edge of the ring. Now click the visibility eye next to the alpha channel to hide it and click back on the RGB channel.

4 Go to **Filter > Blur > Lens Blur**. After the dialog box opens, hold down the Alt/Opt key on the keyboard and click Reset to revert to default values. Check the Preview box and choose Alpha 1 from the Depth Map Source box. This will use the previously created alpha channel to determine where the area of focus lies. Click the Invert box to invert the channel.

5 To control the degree of blur in the out-of-focus areas, slowly drag the Iris Radius slider to the right until you're happy with the degree of blur in those areas. Here, I used a value of 68 for a dramatic effect. The point of focus can be moved with the Blur Focal Distance slider.

6 It helps if a little noise is added to the blur, so set the Amount slider in the Noise panel to 16, and select Uniform for Distribution. Click the OK button. Be patient—the filter can take quite a while to render.

7 Compared with the previous Gaussian Blur effect, this impression of selective focus is much more effective and looks more realistic. Although this process is a little more complicated, the results justify the effort.

Movement and motion blur effects

Some of the most enigmatic and compelling images are those which freeze movement in one area of the image while making the most of the abstract qualities of figures in motion. Dance is an ideal subject for this kind of effect, where a relatively slow shutter speed will render stationary figures sharply, but dancers in motion are rendered as soft, abstract shapes. However, this effect need not be confined to the moment when the camera shutter clicks, as we can replicate the effect in Photoshop with a greater degree of control.

The essential technique consists mainly of making accurate selections via Quick Mask mode and making maximum use of Photoshop's Blur filters. We can carefully combine each of these filter effects via layer masks for ultimate control. In this project, we're using a Smart Filter version of the Motion Blur filter. The advantage here is that if you want a little more—or perhaps less—of a blur, once you've applied the filter you can easily change the settings simply by double-clicking the filter's entry in the Layers palette.

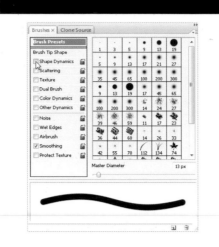

1 With the source image open, hit Q on the keyboard to enter Quick Mask mode. Choose the Brush tool, click in the Brush picker, and select a standard, hard-edged, round brush. Hit F5 to open the Brush Options palette and uncheck the box for the Shape Dynamics category.

3 Hit Q again to exit Quick Mask mode and save this selection, using **Select > Save Selection**. Name the selection "Figure." Hit Ctrl/ Cmd+D on the keyboard to deselect.

2 Ensure that black is your foreground color and paint the red Quick Mask over the dancer on the left of the image. To paint the mask over more intricate parts, reduce the size of the brush with the square bracket keys on the keyboard. Take great care to accurately mask out the figure, diligently following the outlines.

4 To begin constructing the motion blur effect, right-click the Background layer and choose Duplicate Layer. Name this layer "Motion Blur." Go to **Filter > Noise > Add Noise**. In the Noise dialog, choose Monochromatic and Gaussian, setting the Noise amount to 13. Reload the saved selection by going to **Select > Load Selection**, choosing Figure from the Channels box. Hit the Backspace key on the keyboard to delete the main figure from this layer.

5 Press Ctrl/Cmd+D to deselect, and go to **Filter > Convert For Smart Filters**. Then go to **Filter > Blur > Motion Blur**. Make sure that the Preview box is checked, and set the Angle to 0 and the Distance to 193. Go to **Select > Reselect**. Choose the Brush tool and make sure that black is your foreground color. Click on the layer mask for the Smart Filter in the Layers palette and paint with black inside the selection.

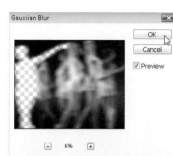

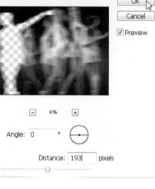

7 With white as your foreground color, choose the Brush tool and a soft brush from the picker. Paint with this brush at a low opacity onto the mask to reveal some of this blur layer just over the girls' heads and limbs. This will add a little more focus here and there.

8 Go to **Layers > Merge Down** to merge the two Blur layers. Add a layer mask to this layer via **Layer > Add Layer Mask > Reveal All**. Using the same brush, paint with black onto the mask around the area where the dancers' hands are linked, to reveal just a little of the sharp Background layer.

Tip

QUICK MASK MODE
In Quick Mask mode (activated by hitting Q on the keyboard), selections can be made by painting a temporary red-tinted mask over the areas you wish to select. By double-clicking the Quick Mask icon below the foreground and background color swatches, you can decide whether your painted mask relates to Masked or Selected areas.
Once you exit Quick Mask mode, it's a good idea to save the selection, using **Select > Save Selection**. Using this same dialog box, you can also change the color of the temporary Quick Mask overlay, which makes painting the mask a bit easier on some images, particularly those with a lot of red tones.

6 Click again on the Background layer, and choose Duplicate Layer. Drag the new layer to the top of the stack and reload the saved Figure selection.

Hit the Backspace key, and go to **Filter > Blur > Gaussian Blur**, using a radius of 25. Add a layer mask, by going to **Layer > Add Layer Mask > Hide All**.

133

Cloning with perspective

We're used to using Photoshop's cloning tools for repairing images, but when those images include dramatic perspectives it can be very difficult to clone convincingly, as the area you're cloning from often does not have the same perspective as the area you're cloning to. Here, we've got just such a situation, where we need to replace a couple of windows while keeping the integrity of the perspective. Thankfully, in CS3, we have a tool that is designed for this task: the Vanishing Point command. The Vanishing Point command is so impressive that you'll never tire of using it. By first defining the perspective plane, you can actually clone from one area of the building to another and Photoshop will cope with the perspective on the fly, melding the cloned areas seamlessly with the existing lines of perspective.

1 Open the start image and add a new layer (Ctrl/Cmd+Shift+N). To begin cloning with perspective, go to **Filter > Vanishing Point**.

Once you're in the Vanishing Point workspace, choose the Zoom tool and zoom in to the building so the upper floor fills the screen.

2 From the Vanishing Point toolbar, choose the Create Plane tool. Starting at the top left corner of the upper floor, click the first point of the perspective grid. Drag the top line of the grid

along the top line of the building, making sure that it runs in line with the stone work. Then, click at the other corner to place another grid point.

3 By moving the mouse, lay the next perspective plane edge down the corner line of the building, clicking another point where the upper floor meets the lower.

4 To complete the plane, drag to the lower left corner and click there. Your perspective plane will now appear. Be sure that the grid is lined up with all of the building's edges and that it is blue, indicating accurate perspective. A yellow or red

grid indicates an inaccurate plane. If things are not quite in line, choose the Edit Plane tool and drag on the points to correct the plane to line it up perfectly with the perspective of the building.

5 We need to wrap this plane of perspective around the building, so place your mouse pointer over the right-hand, middle handle on the plane. Your pointer will change to a double-ended arrow. Hold down the Ctrl/Cmd key and drag

to the far right side of the upper floor. An extension of this plane will appear on the other side of the building, conforming to the same perspective. Again, you can use the Edit Plane tool to adjust the plane if needed.

Tip

CLONE STAMP TOOL
We've cloned by making selections here, but you can also clone within the Vanishing Point filter as you would normally, using the Clone Stamp tool. Of course, the major difference is that once you've created your perspective plane, the Clone Stamp will clone with Perspective. The tool works in the same way as the conventional Clone Stamp; simply Alt-Click to set your clone source point and clone away!

134

6 Now that the planes of perspective are complete, any cloning we do within the Vanishing Point workspace will conform to the same perspective. Select the Marquee tool; unlike the conventional Marquee tool, this one will draw selections that actually conform to the perspective set by the plane you've just created. Drag a selection around the outside of the third window across on the right side of the building. Ensure that Move Mode is set to Destination.

8 Now, choose the Transform tool from the Toolbar. Adjust the handles around the selection to fit the window exactly into the space. Click back on the Marquee tool and eliminate any hard outlines by adjusting the Feather value in the Options bar, softening the edges of the cloned area. Return the opacity to 100%.

10 Click and hold within the selection and drag the selection over the window next to it until the new window sits in the space precisely. Release the mouse button when you're happy and click OK to apply the Vanishing Point filter.

7 We need to make a floating selection to use to clone over the open window. In Options, set the opacity to 60%, hold down the Alt key, and click and drag within the selection. Keep the mouse button held down and position the cloned window over the open one next to it. You can easily line things up, as the clone source is set to 60% opacity. When you're happy with the positioning, release the mouse button and set Heal to On in the options.

9 For the blank window on the other side of the building, we'll use another mode. Again, choose the Marquee tool and drag a selection around the outside of the blank window. From the Move Mode box, choose Source.

Creating panoramas

nless you have a very expensive, super-wide-angle lens and a very large format camera, creating panoramic images will mean you need to stitch together a number of sequential but separate images. There was a time when this was a decidedly manual and very complicated process using Photoshop, with a stitching plug-in. However, Photoshop CS3 features the much-improved Photomerge command, which takes much of the trouble out of the process. Panoramas can now be created in a couple of mouse clicks.

The panorama itself can be made up of as many separate images as you wish; here, we're using just three. Follow the recipe and discover just how easy panoramas are with Photoshop CS3!

1 Panoramas are surprisingly easy to create in Photoshop CS3, and the Photomerge command is much improved from CS2. It's now a largely automated process. To begin, open all of the images that will be used in the final panoramic picture. Remember that it's important that the content of each image overlaps with the next.

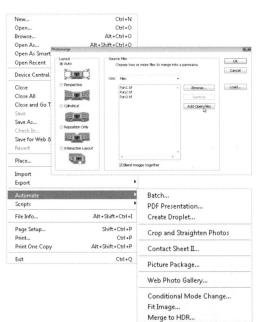

2 The Photomerge command is buried in the File menu, so go to **File > Automate > Photomerge**. The first dialog gives you the opportunity to choose the individual files that will make up the final panorama. To choose the files you've opened, simply hit the Add Open Files button. Make sure that Blend Images Together is checked.

3 Often, the best layout option to choose is Auto, as CS3 does a very good job of fitting the images together and correcting exposure differences between each image. Click OK to begin the Photomerge process.

4 You will now see Photoshop reading and placing each file, which may take a while, depending on the speed of your computer and the size of the files. Once Photoshop completes the process, it will display your merged panorama.

Tip

IMAGES FOR PANORAMAS
When you're out with your camera and shooting the source images for your panorama, remember that it's vital to put your camera on a tripod. The better the features in the images line up with each other, the more success Photoshop will have at stitching them together. By using a tripod, you can pan the scene between shots, ensuring that the camera remains at the same level throughout the entire series of images.

5 You'll now see a number of layers in the Layers palette. There's one layer, complete with a layer mask, for each of your original images. Before moving on, go to **Layer** > **Merge Visible**, to merge all three layers together.

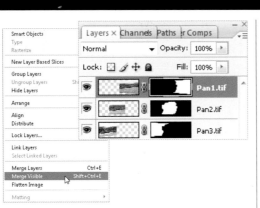

7 Choose the Crop tool from the Toolbar and click and drag over the entire image. Adjust the handles around the crop box to crop out any transparent or ragged areas around the edges of the image. Double-click within the image to apply the crop.

8 Finally, adjust the Levels for the image, using **Image** > **Adjustments** > **Levels**. Ensure that the black pointer is directly below the left-hand end of the histogram.

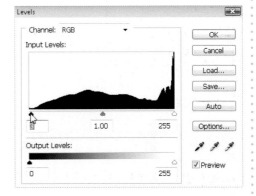

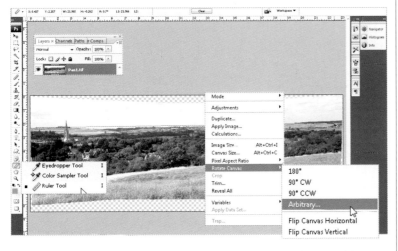

6 The completed panorama will invariably need cropping and tidying up a little, but first it's often necessary to adjust the level of the horizon line. Click and hold on the Eyedropper tool and choose the Ruler tool from the fly-out. Click on the horizon line on the left, hold down the mouse button, and drag to the other end of the horizon. Go to **Image** > **Rotate Canvas** > **Arbitrary** and click OK to correct the level.

Adding Tattoos

If you've always hankered after a really good tattoo, but the thought of all of that pain has put you off, Photoshop CS3 has the solution. Here, we're going to look at how to apply a convincing tattoo to an image.

We've supplied the initial tattoo design, but you could just as easily create one for yourself by using the Pen tool and filling a path with color. What's most impressive about this technique is the new Clone Source capability of CS3, where we can clone an image from one file to another. You might not think that's so impressive, but you'll soon see that, thanks to Clone Source, you can not only clone, but you can also scale and rotate the source image to your heart's content before any actual cloning takes place. Now that's cloning at its best!

Of course, for a tattoo to look convincing, it needs to conform to the body it's applied to. To do that we'll be using the Warp command and Liquify filter. Follow the recipe and discover how to get tattooed, without the pain!

1 Open tattoo_design.jpg. Choose the Magic Wand tool from the Toolbar, set the Tolerance to 10, and check both Anti Alias and Contiguous. Click on the Add To Selection icon, then click in the white area of the image with the wand to select it. Shift-click the white diamond shape at the center of the design to add it to the selection.

2 Go to **Select > Inverse**, followed by **Layer > New > Layer Via Copy**. In the Layers palette, click the visibility eye for the Background layer to hide it.

3 Choose the Clone Stamp tool and go to **Window > Clone Source** to display the Clone Source palette. Hold down the Alt/Opt key and click the center of the design to set the Clone Source point. You'll see the document filename displayed as the first Source Point in the Clone Source palette. Open the figure image and add a new layer (Ctrl-Shift-N). Make sure that Aligned is turned off in the Options bar. In the Clone Source palette, check the Show Overlay option.

4 You'll now see a ghost of your source image, which you can drag around with your mouse. Position the tattoo so it sits roughly over the model's navel and click to set the position. Go to the Options bar and check the Aligned box.

5 To resize and rotate the tattoo, highlight the Angle value in the Clone Source palette, then hold down the Shift key and hit the up arrow key on the keyboard until the angle of the design matches the model's torso.

6 Highlight the W Scale value and use the down arrow key until the size of the tattoo is about right for the body. Here, we've settled on a value of 78%. Highlight the X Offset value and adjust it using the arrow keys until the design is centered above the navel.

7 Increase the size of the brush for the Clone Stamp tool and begin to paint over the ghosted source image to clone the design onto the new layer. Name the upper layer "Cloned Tattoo" and set its blending mode to Multiply, and the opacity to 75%.

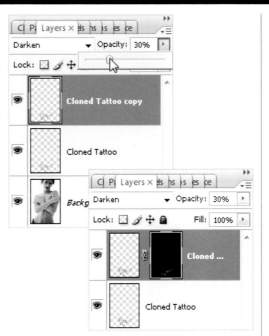

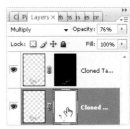

8 On the Tattoo layer, go to **Edit > Transform > Warp**. The aim here is to fit the tattoo to the contours of the model's torso. You can warp the tattoo by dragging the Warp mesh. Do this a little at a time, using the screenshot as a guide. When you're done, click OK.

9 Choose the Eraser tool and a hard, round brush from the Brush Picker. Erase any areas of the tattoo which fall outside the body, or over the arms.

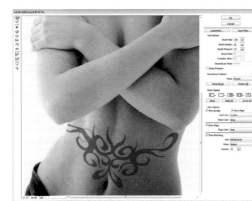

10 For finer adjustments we'll use the Liquify filter, so go to **Filter>Liquify**. In the Liquify workspace, choose the Forward Warp tool. In the lower right area of the dialog, check the boxes for Show Image, Show Mesh, and Show Backdrop. Set the Brush size to 100, Brush Density to 26, and Pressure to 25. Gently push the design around the muscles on the torso, using the screenshot as a guide. Click OK to apply the filter.

11 Duplicate the Tattoo layer and set the blending mode of the duplicate layer to Darken, reducing the opacity to 30%. Add a layer mask, using **Layer > Layer Mask > Hide All**. Ensure that white is your foreground color, then choose the Brush tool and a soft brush. Reduce the opacity of the brush to 25%.

12 Click on the layer mask and carefully paint over the areas of the tattoo that are over shaded areas of the model's torso. This will make these areas of the tattoo darker. Because you're using the brush at a low opacity, the effect is quite subtle, but will accentuate the form.

13 Select the lower tattoo layer and add a layer mask using **Layer > Layer Mask > Reveal All**. Ensure that your foreground color is black and paint on the layer mask over the lighter areas of the torso. This will lighten these areas of the tattoo and enhance the contours.

14 Click each layer mask in turn, choosing Apply Layer Mask. Then click on the upper tattoo layer and go to **Layer > Merge Down**. On the newly merged layer, choose the Blur tool from the Toolbar. In the Options bar, set the Strength to 20%. Use this tool around the edges of the tattoo to soften them a little here and there, particularly on the far side of the body.

TEXTURE EFFECTS

Using texture overlays

With Photoshop as our image-editing tool of choice, we're not limited to producing smooth-toned and flawless images. By using textures, we can apply convincing effects of weathered surfaces and peeling paint. It's really useful to build up a good collection of texture images to use in such projects, and there are always many opportunities to grab some texture shots with a digital camera. There are also many places on the Web where royalty-free texture shots are available.

In this project, we'll create a convincing weather-beaten inn sign with realistic surface textures.

1 Open the horse image. We need to make the current background layer editable, so double-click it in the Layers palette, and name the new layer "Horse" in the dialog box.

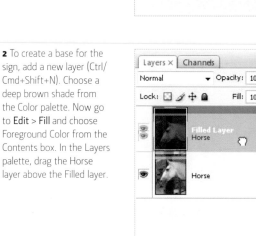

2 To create a base for the sign, add a new layer (Ctrl/Cmd+Shift+N). Choose a deep brown shade from the Color palette. Now go to **Edit** > **Fill** and choose Foreground Color from the Contents box. In the Layers palette, drag the Horse layer above the Filled layer.

3 Open the Boards image and go to **Select** > **All** (Ctrl/Cmd+A). Choose **Edit** > **Copy** (Ctrl/Cmd+C). Close this image. Working on the main composition, go to **Edit** > **Paste** (Ctrl/Cmd+V) to paste a copy of the Boards image into the main composition. We need to stretch this layer so that it covers the entire image, so go to **Edit** > **Transform** > **Scale**. Holding down the Shift key to retain the proportions, drag on the handles at the corners of the bounding box to stretch the Boards image. Hit the Commit checkmark in the Options bar to apply the transformation. Set the blending mode to Hard Light and reduce the opacity to 40%.

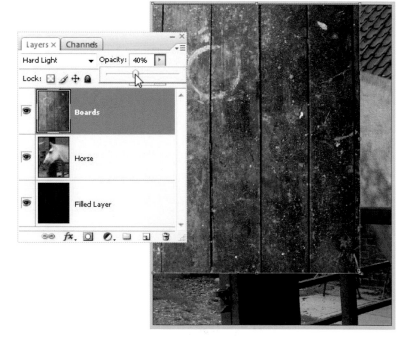

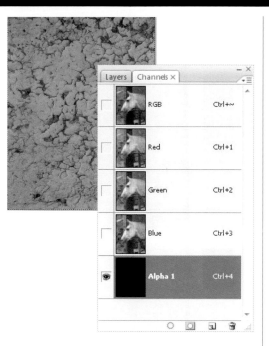

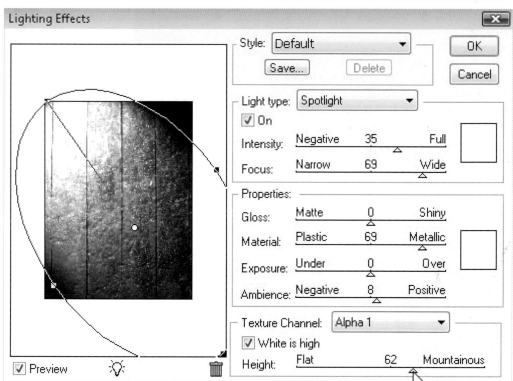

Lighting Effects

Style: Default

Save... Delete

OK
Cancel

Light type: Spotlight

☑ On

Intensity: Negative   35   Full

Focus: Narrow   69   Wide

Properties:

Gloss: Matte   0   Shiny

Material: Plastic   69   Metallic

Exposure: Under   0   Over

Ambience: Negative   8   Positive

Texture Channel: Alpha 1

☑ White is high

Height: Flat   62   Mountainous

☑ Preview

4 Open the Rough Paint image and go to **Select** > **All** (Ctrl/Cmd+A), followed by **Edit** > **Copy** (Ctrl/Cmd+C). Close this image and return to the main composition. Click on the Channels palette tab and choose the "Create new channel" icon at the base of the palette.

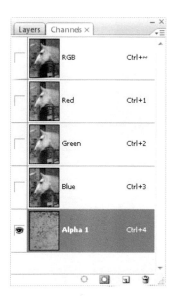

5 Working on the new channel, go to **Edit** > **Paste** (Ctrl/Cmd+V). Fit this rough paint texture to the image, using **Edit** > **Transform** > **Scale** as described in step 3.

After applying the transformation, click on the RGB channel in the Channels palette and then return to the Layers palette.

6 Right-click/Ctrl-click the Boards layer and choose Duplicate Layer We're going to light this layer using the alpha channel we just created as the texture reference. Go to **Filter** > **Render** > **Lighting Effects**. Rotate the Light Pool in the Preview box with the outer handles so the lightest part sits at the top left of the image. Drag on the side handles so the light pool covers the entire width of the image. From the Texture Channel box, choose Alpha 1. Experiment with the other sliders to the best effect, or replicate the settings shown in the screenshot. Click OK and set this layer's blending mode to Overlay, with an opacity of 50%.

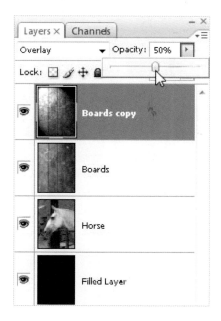

143

Using texture overlays continued

8 Return to the Boards copy layer, right-click/Ctrl-click it, and choose Duplicate Layer. Drag this layer down the layer stack until it sits directly below the Horse layer. Set the opacity of this layer to 83% and change the blending mode to Normal.

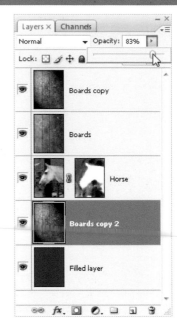

7 Now, we'll hide some of the main Horse layer. Click on the Horse layer, and add a layer mask, using **Layer > Layer Mask > Reveal All**. Choose the Brush tool, click in the Brush Picker, and hit the right-pointing arrow, selecting Reset Brushes. Choose Dry Brush from the brush thumbnails and paint around the horse's head with black. We're painting onto the mask to hide the unwanted background areas and reveal the Filled layer underneath. Use this brush at 80% opacity (set in the Options bar) so that it leaves just a trace of the surrounding background detail showing here and there.

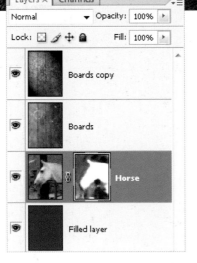

9 To add the lettering, choose the Horizontal Text tool. Click on the top layer in the Layers palette and then click to add text at the bottom of the image. Type the text and choose a typeface from the picker in the Options bar. Adjust the type size using the Font Size box, and choose a suitable color from the Text Color box. Hit the Commit checkmark to apply the text.

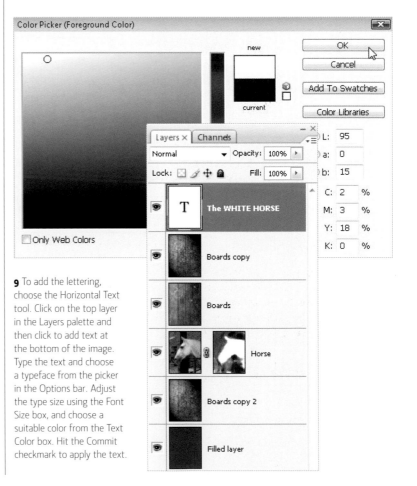

144

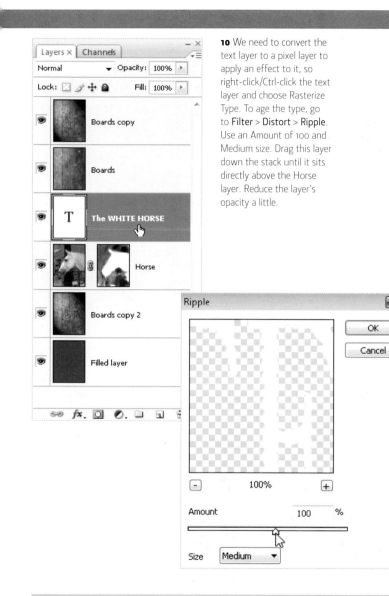

10 We need to convert the text layer to a pixel layer to apply an effect to it, so right-click/Ctrl-click the text layer and choose Rasterize Type. To age the type, go to **Filter** > **Distort** > **Ripple**. Use an Amount of 100 and Medium size. Drag this layer down the stack until it sits directly above the Horse layer. Reduce the layer's opacity a little.

145

11 If desired, it's easy to create another line of text using the same method.

Tip

THE LIGHTING EFFECTS FILTER

The majority of adjustments within the filter dialog box take place within the preview window. First, make sure that the Preview box is checked, so you can gauge the effect as you make adjustments. The circle with the handles around it denotes the pool of light, with the highest concentration of light along the axis line bisecting the pool. The light can be moved by clicking and dragging the central spot, and the light pool can be widened by pulling on the outer handles. The rake of the light is controlled by using the handles that sit in line with the axis. The Light Type and Properties sliders control the intensity of the light and the effect it has on the subject.

Turning a figure to stone

I t's the stuff of legends: a witch turns an unsuspecting maiden to stone with a flick of her magic wand. In Photoshop, we can cast a similar spell, taking an ordinary digital image and using powerful layer blending mode features and a few layer masks to transform a figure into a stone statue.

This effect is all about how multiple layers combine and meld together. We can make these layer blending properties even more sophisticated by selectively controlling the opacity with layer masks. This technique makes extensive use of the extra brush sets, which has brushes that are very effective for expressing textures within the stroke.

1 This image, with the praying position of the model, lends itself well to this effect, and is already quite statuesque. Start by duplicating the background layer (**Layer > Duplicate Layer**), as this preserves a pristine copy of the image at the bottom of the layer stack. Desaturate the duplicate layer by going to **Image > Adjustments > Desaturate** (Ctrl/Cmd+Shift+U).

2 To increase the contrast, go to **Image > Adjustments > Curves** and replicate the curve shape in the screenshot. This curve shape lightens the midtones and highlights and darkens the shadows.

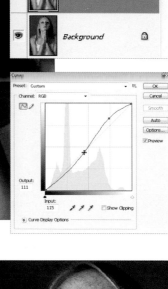

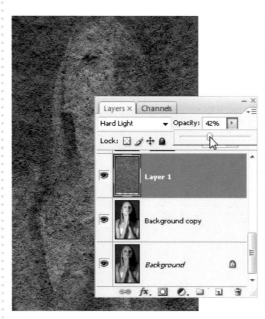

3 Open an image of a stone surface, and go to **Select > All** (Ctrl/Cmd+A), then **Edit > Copy** (Ctrl/Cmd+C) to copy the entire image. Return to the main composition and go to **Edit > Paste** (Ctrl/Cmd+V).

Stretch this stone layer to cover the entire figure, using **Edit > Transform > Scale** and dragging the corner handles to fit. Set the blending mode for this layer to Hard Light, and the opacity to 42%.

4 Add a layer mask to the Stone layer using **Layer > Layer Mask > Reveal All**. Use the Brush tool to paint around the girl's head and shoulders with black onto the layer mask to hide the stone texture in these areas.

5 Open a second, rougher stone image and copy and paste it into the main composition as above. Resize this layer, using **Edit > Transform > Scale** so it covers just the head and upper arms. Set the blending mode to Hard Light and opacity to 58%. Add a layer mask and paint with black around the head as in step 4.

6 Return to the background copy layer in the Layers palette and choose the Dodge tool from the Toolbar. In the Options bar, set the Range to Shadows and the Exposure to 23%. Click with the tool over the girl's eyes to lighten the tone of the pupils.

Range: Shadows | Exposure: 23% |

7 Change to the Healing Brush tool and clone out the highlights in the eyes. Set the clone source point by first Alt/Opt-clicking next to the highlight.

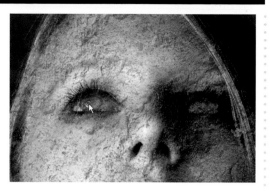

8 Choose the Eyedropper tool and click to sample one of the highlights in the hair. Then go to **Select > Color Range** and move the Fuzziness slider to 53. Hit OK and go to **Edit > Copy** (Ctrl/Cmd+C), then **Edit > Paste** (Ctrl/Cmd+V) to paste the highlights onto a separate layer.

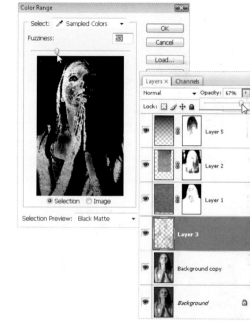

Tip

LAYER MASKS

It's as simple as black and white. Layer masks can be confusing at first, but don't be put off. Think of a layer mask as an invisible grayscale overlay, where black hides the associated image layer and white reveals it. A Reveal All mask is filled with white, and, as a consequence, the entire layer is visible. Conversely, a Hide All mask is filled with black. When you paint with black at low opacity (or light pressure with a stylus) onto a Reveal All mask, the brushstrokes make that part of the mask layer partially opaque, so that the associated image layer only partially shows through. It's vital to make sure you're painting onto the layer mask and not the layer itself. You can check this by looking for a bold outline around the thumbnail for the mask in the Layers palette and for the mask symbol in the Layers palette margin.

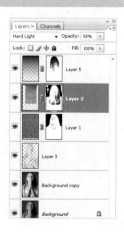

Turning a figure to stone continued

9 Blur this layer by going to Filter > Blur > Gaussian Blur, using a radius value of 28. This will give the image a softer appearance. A higher radius value can be used to make the effect more subtle. Reduce the layer opacity to 67%.

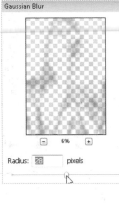

11 To light the figure, go to Filter > Render > Lighting Effects. Choose Spotlight, and for the Texture Channel, choose Alpha 1. Rotate the light direction pool in the Preview window so the light falls from the top left. Use the settings in the screenshot as a guide for the other values. Hit OK. Set the layer blending mode to Luminosity, and the opacity to 45%.

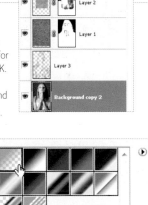

10 Click on the background copy layer and duplicate it (Ctrl/Cmd+J). Go to Select > All (Ctrl/Cmd+A), Edit > Copy (Ctrl/Cmd+C), and Ctrl/Cmd+D to deselect. Now click on the Channels palette tab and click the "Create new channel" icon at the bottom of the palette. Go to Edit > Paste (Ctrl/Cmd+V) to paste the contents of the new duplicate layer into the alpha channel. Blur this channel with Filter > Blur > Gaussian Blur, using a radius of 5.2. Click on the RGB channel before returning to the Layers palette.

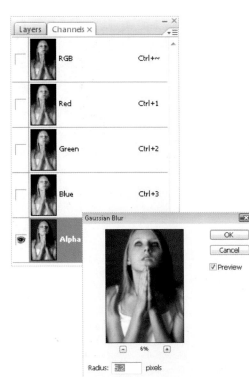

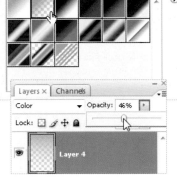

12 Click on the foreground color swatch and select a light blue from the Color Picker. Add a new layer (Ctrl/Cmd+Shift+ N) and drag it to the top of the layer stack. Choose the Gradient tool and Foreground to Transparent in the Gradient Picker. Click and drag from the top to the bottom. Set the layer blending mode to Color and opacity to 46%.

148

13 Click on the layer mask thumbnail attached to the upper stone layer and choose the Brush tool. Click in the Brush Picker and on the small, right-pointing arrow. Load the Dry Media Brush set from the list and choose the Pastel Rough Texture Brush from the thumbnails.

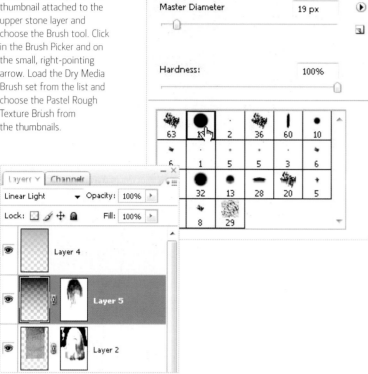

14 If you're using a graphics tablet, hit F5 to display the Brush Options dialog box and click in the Other Dynamics category. For Opacity Jitter choose Pen Pressure. Ensure that Shape Dynamics is not checked.

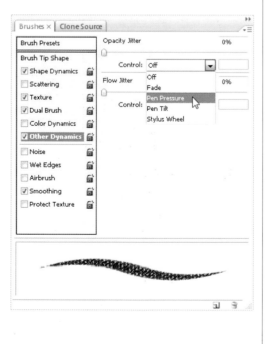

15 Paint with black at varying opacities on the layer mask in the darkest areas of the girl's head and shoulders to obliterate some of the stone texture. Paint with black into the mask around any edges of the stone layer to hide them.

149

16 Repeat step 15 on the layer mask for the lower stone layer, paying special attention to the edges of the visible layer. Paint around these edges, using black at a very low opacity to carefully blend this layer into the figure. Refer to the Layer Masks box on page 147 for more tips.

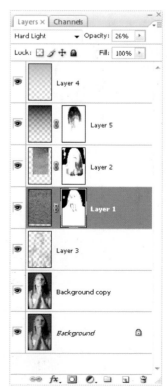

Turning a figure to stone continued

17 Now to add some drama to the image. Add a new layer (Ctrl/Cmd+Shift+N) and drag it below the blue gradient layer. Choose a very dark blue for the foreground swatch and select the Gradient tool. Drag a gradient over the entire image from top to bottom. Change the blending mode for this layer to Linear Light.

18 Add a layer mask to this layer, using **Layer > Layer Mask > Reveal All**. Make sure you're working on the mask for this layer by checking for an outline around the thumbnail.

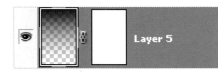

19 Choose the Brush tool and use the previously selected brush to paint black into the mask at varying opacities over the entire upper half of the figure. Paint at higher opacity over the left side of the face to give the impression of light falling on that side. Reduce the brush opacity (or use less pressure on your stylus) on the other side of the face to subtly reveal parts of the face.

20 Add another layer (Ctrl/Cmd+Shift+N) and set the layer blending mode to Color. Change the foreground swatch color to dark green and paint here and there over the head at very low opacity to add a little color. Repeat this process using a rich brown color.

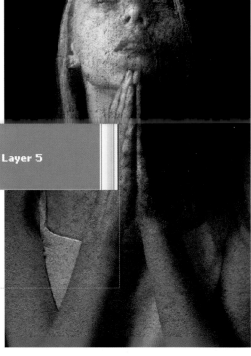

21 Flatten the image (**Layer > Flatten Image**) and use the Healing Brush tool to clone out the edges of the tank top. Choose the Healing Brush tool, press Alt/Opt on the keyboard, and click at a point next to the edge of the girl's top to set the Healing Brush source point. Release the Alt/Opt key and click along the edges of the top to hide them.

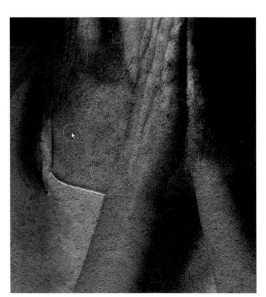

150

22 Finally, add one more new layer. Choose the Polygon Lasso tool and draw a wedge shape in the top left-hand corner for the light beam. Using light blue for the foreground color, drag a gradient diagonally across the selection. Change the layer blending mode to Screen and reduce the layer opacity.

Wood textures

To create a wood texture we'll look at a method which uses Photoshop's Layer Styles. Layer Styles supply a quick route to a texture, but are limited as far as being able to customize the effect, so we'll emphasize the texture and add some realism with the Lighting Effects filter. Ultimately, these textures can be used for everything from texturizing type, to making virtual surfaces suitable for use as a base in a still-life.

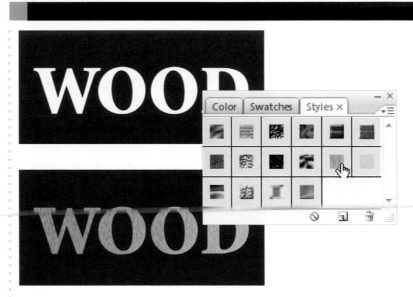

1 Here, as an example of how to use a wood Layer Style, I've added some type to a layer, which we'll now turn into wood. To create the text, simply use the Horizontal Type tool over a filled Background Layer.

2 Here you can see the plain text on a separate layer. To create the first wood effect we'll apply a Style to this layer. Working on the Type layer, go to **Window > Styles** to display the Styles palette. Right-click the small right-pointing arrow in the palette and load the extures styles set. Choose Oak from the Style swatches to apply the texture to the type.

3 Double-click on the Effects panel attached to the type layer to modify the size of the grain in the wood. Select the Pattern Overlay category in the Layer Styles dialog and adjust the scale. Choose the Color Overlay category to change the color of the wood effect by choosing another overlay color.

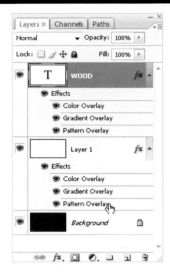

4 Here I've added another layer below the text. I filled it with white and applied the same style. After double-clicking the effects panel for this layer, another color was chosen for the color overlay to create a parquetry effect, where two different kinds of wood are combined.

5 Flatten the image via **Layer > Flatten Image**. Next, we'll apply some lighting, using this image as an alpha channel for added effect. Go to **Select > All** and then to **Edit>Copy** (Ctrl/Cmd+C) Click on the tab for the Channels palette and add a new channel via the New Channel icon at the base of the channel. This will add an alpha channel, initially filled with black.

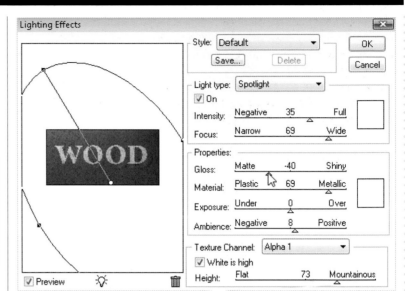

6 Now, go to **Edit > Paste** (Ctrl/Cmd+V) to paste the image copy into this alpha channel. Return to the Layers palette, and click on the Background Layer. Go to **Filter > Convert For Smart Filters**.To apply the lighting, go to **Filter >** **Render > Lighting Effects**. In the Lighting Effects dialog, click in the Texture Channel box and choose Alpha 1 (the pasted wood texture). The Height slider determines how obvious the texture will be, so set this to 73 for a fairly heavy texture.

153

Tip

THE TYPE TOOL

Using the Type tool is as simple as clicking and typing. You don't need to add a new layer for type, Photoshop does it automatically. As soon as you've typed your words, you can choose a font face and a size for the type from the Options bar—simply click in the relevant boxes and make your changes. Remember, when your type is complete, you need to click the Commit checkmark in the Options bar to apply the text.

7 We want the surface of the wood to be fairly matte in appearance, so set the Gloss Properties slider to −40. Finally, drag on the sliders around the light pool in the Preview pane to position the light. Position the light by dragging the central spot in the pool, then click OK to apply the lighting and texture. As you can see, the added effect of applying the texture via an alpha channel in the Lighting Effects dialog makes the finished wood texture far more convincing.

Stone texture

Here we'll look at the texture of stone, which by its very nature has a random quality to it. If you've followed many of the recipes in this book, you'll know that the best tool for creating a random pattern is the Clouds filter, and we'll use this filter again here. We'll also employ an alpha channel, in conjunction with the Lighting Effects filter, giving us the ability to simulate a very realistic surface.

We'll even add some lettering, carved into the stone here, giving an added touch of realism with a couple of applied layer styles.

This stone texture, like the rest of the textures in this section, can be used to add an extra touch of magic to your Photoshop composite images!

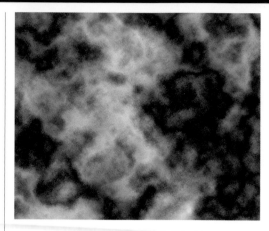

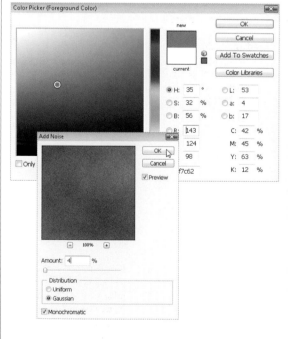

1 To begin creating the carved stone effect, we'll start with a new document. Here I've made a new document measuring 3 inches square at 200 dpi.

It's best to keep your file size fairly small for this effect; you can always resize the final flattened image to suit your needs.

2 On the blank white file, click on the tab for the Channels palette. Add a new channel to the image via the Create New Channel button at the base of the palette. The channel will be named Alpha 1. We'll create the texture map for the stone effect here.

4 Go to **Filter > Render > Difference Clouds** to create a more random texture. Re-apply this filter a few times by returning to the Filter menu (Difference Clouds will be the first entry in the menu, as it was the last used). Re-apply the filter until you have a suitably intricate texture. Here I've applied the filter a total of 4 times.

3 Working on the alpha channel, hit D to revert to default black/white colors and go to **Filter > Render > Clouds**. This will give us a random fill to begin the effect. Now, add some noise to this Clouds fill via **Filter > Noise > Add Noise**. Use an Amount of 6%, choosing Gaussian and Monochromatic.

5 Return to the Layers palette and click on the original Background Layer. Working on the blank document, choose a dark gray for the foreground color and a warm light gray/ brown for the background color. Now, go to **Filter > Render > Clouds**. Again, add some noise to the clouds via **Filter > Noise > Add Noise**, using an Amount of 4%.

6 We'll light this layer, using the alpha channel as a texture map. Go to **Filter > Convert For Smart Filters**, then go to **Filter > Render > Lighting Effects**. Position the light pool by rotating it, so the light falls from the top left. Set the Intensity to 35, Focus to 69. Choose Alpha 1 (the channel we created earlier) from the Texture Channel box. Set the Height slider to 76. You can experiment with the setting in the Properties section. Hit OK to apply the lighting. Now we've got a very realistic-looking stone surface.

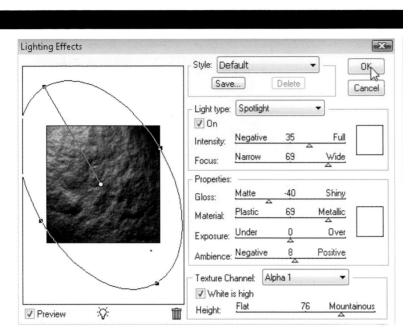

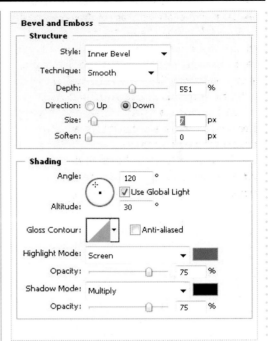

7 To add the chiselled lettering to the stone, choose the Horizontal Type tool from the Toolbar. Click in the image, and type your words, using a suitable font. Adjust the size of the font in the Options bar. Click the Commit tick in the Options bar to generate a selection from the type.

9 To add the finishing touch, duplicate the pasted type layer. Right-click the Effects panel on the new layer and choose Clear Layer Style. Go to **Layer > Layer Style > Bevel and Emboss**. For the Style, choose Inner Bevel. Check the Preview checkbox and set the Depth and Size sliders to values of your choice. Click OK to apply the style. Set the blending mode for this layer to Hue in the Layers palette.

8 With the selection active, go to **Select > Refine Edge**, using a feather radius of 2 pixels. Now, go to **Edit > Copy** (Ctrl/Cmd+C) followed by **Edit > Paste** (Ctrl/Cmd+V) to copy and paste the selected type. On this pasted layer, go to **Layer > Layer Style > Inner Shadow**. Set the Angle to 120, Distance to 13, Choke to 32, and the Size to 24. This will create the effect of chiselled lettering.

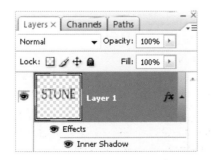

Metal effect

Another texture effect that has many uses is metal. Using metal textures as backgrounds or as part of a composition can add unusual and interesting effects.

Once again, we'll use a combination of layers and the powerful Lighting Effects filter. We also need to create an alpha channel, which will act as a texture map for the contours of the surface when we throw light across it within the filter. This gives the end product that 3-dimensional appearance that transforms a fairly simple texture into a convincingly realistic surface. We could even use the virtual surface for a background in a modern portrait image, throwing a shadow from the figure onto a metal background.

1 First, we'll create an alpha channel, which will ultimately stamp the lettering into the metal plate. Create a new document via **File > New**. Here, I've made a document 5 inches square at a resolution of 250 dpi. In the new document, choose the Horizontal Type tool from the Toolbar. Click in the blank document and type the word "Metal." From the Options bar, choose Impact for the Type (font) and adjust the size.

2 We need to blur the type a little so that it has an embossed effect on the metal. Go to **Filter > Blur > Gaussian Blur**, answering OK to the Rasterize Type Layer dialog. Use a Blur Radius of 4 pixels and click OK. Flatten the image via **Layer > Flatten Image**.

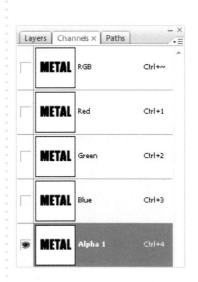

3 We need to copy this image to an alpha channel, so go to **Select > All**, followed by **Edit > Copy** (Ctrl/Cmd+C). Now, click the tab for the Channels palette and hit the Create New Channel button at its base. Then go to **Edit > Paste** (Ctrl/Cmd+V) to paste the image into the alpha channel. Click the tab for the Layers palette and click on the Background Layer.

4 To create the metal base, choose a mid blue/gray for the foreground color and a lighter shade for the background. Select the Gradient tool from the Toolbar. Click in the Gradient Picker, choosing Foreground to Background from the swatches. Choose Reflected Gradient from the Options bar, then click and drag the gradient from the center of the canvas to the upper left corner.

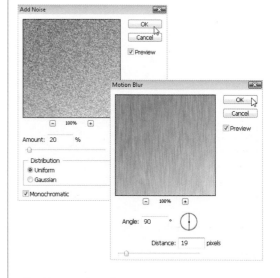

5 To add some grain to the metal, go to **Filter > Noise > Add Noise**. Use an Amount of 20%, Uniform for Distribution, and check Monochromatic. Go to **Filter > Blur > Motion Blur**, using an Angle of 90 degrees and a Distance of 19.

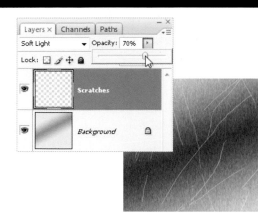

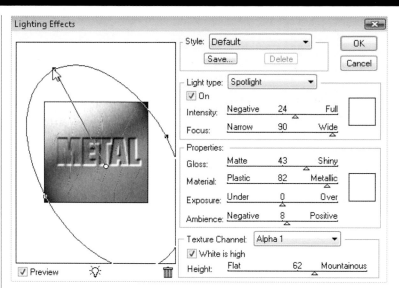

8 Finally, flatten the image via **Layer > Flatten Image**. Now, light the metal plate, embossing it with the previously made alpha channel. Go to **Filter > Convert For Smart Filters**, followed by **Filter > Render > Lighting Effects**. From the Texture Channel box, use Alpha 1 (your type channel) and set the Height slider to 62. In the Preview pane, drag the handles around the light pool to position it, and, in the Properties dialog, set Gloss to 43, Material to 82. Click OK.

6 Now let's add some scratches and imperfections to the metal plate. Add a new layer and set the layer blending mode to Soft Light. Reduce the layer opacity to 70%. Choose the Brush tool from the Toolbar and a very small, hard brush from the Brush Picker. Scribble over the plate, using white to simulate scratches.

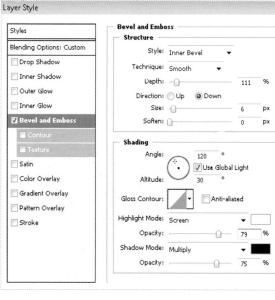

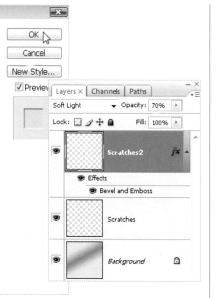

157

Tip

MORE MARKS

In steps 6 and 7, try experimenting with some of Photoshop's other brushes for different kinds of marks and dents in the metal surface. Many of the brushes from the Dry Media brush set (loaded by clicking the small right-pointing arrow in the Brush Picker) will simulate very realistic scuffs and scrapes on the metal surface.

7 Add another new layer with the same blending mode and opacity. Draw more scratches onto this layer. Increase the size of the brush and paint various small blobs here and there over the metal plate to simulate dents in the metal. Try to place these randomly. Add a layer style via **Layer >** Add Layer Style > **Bevel and Emboss**. Choose Inner Bevel from the Style box and experiment with the sliders for the best effect. Here I've used Depth 111, Size 6. Add some noise to this layer via **Filter > Noise > Add Noise** to give the effect of corrosion in the dents.

Glass effect

In this example, we'll create a decorative stained-glass effect. This effect can be used for realistic backgrounds in any Photoshop work—in a portrait or still-life composition, for example. This technique could also be used to create unusual and attractive greetings cards.

Essentially, the technique works by first building a framework representing the lead in a stained-glass window, and then filling the individual cells with color and applying Photoshop's own Glass distortion filter.

1 For this effect, begin with a new document. Go to **File > New**. Set the dimensions of the document—here I've chosen 8 inches by 5 inches. Set the resolution to 300 dpi and choose White for Background Contents.

2 Now, we need to establish the outline for the lettering in the stained-glass panel. Click and hold the Horizontal Type tool, and choose the Horizontal Type Mask tool from the fly-out. The Type Mask tool creates a selection in the shape of the type, rather than solid letters, which is what we need here. Add a new layer (Ctrl/Cmd+Shift+N) and click in the document. Type the line of text and adjust the font and size in the Options bar. Click the Commit checkmark to apply the type selection.

3 To begin creating the lead strips around the glass, go to **Edit > Stroke**, using a Stroke Width of 25 pixels, and Outside for Location. Hit OK. Once the lettering is outlined, hit Ctrl/Cmd+D on the keyboard to deselect. To create a border, go to **Select > All** (Ctrl/Cmd+A) and return to **Edit > Stroke**, choosing Inside for Location. Hit OK, and Ctrl/Cmd+D to deselect.

158

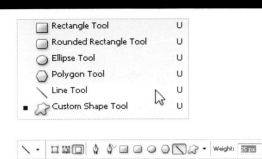

Rectangle Tool	U
Rounded Rectangle Tool	U
Ellipse Tool	U
Polygon Tool	U
Line Tool	U
Custom Shape Tool	U

4 Now, we need to divide the empty white section around the lettering into cells for the various sections of colored glass. Choose the Line tool (which may be nested beneath the currently displayed Shape tool) from the Toolbar, and set the Weight to 25 pixels in the Options bar. Choose the Fill Pixels icon from the far left of the Options.

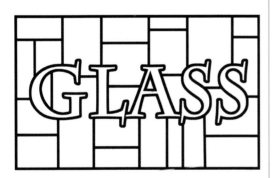

5 Holding down the Shift key on the keyboard, click and drag with this tool from the lettering outward to divide up the empty white space. Feel free to create as few or as many cells as desired. Try to place the lines so that they don't render the lettering illegible

6 Now that we have the framework for the stained-glass panel established, we need to select each cell individually, color it, and apply the glass surface. Duplicate the Framework layer (Ctrl/Cmd+J), renaming the lower layer "Colored Glass." Select the Magic Wand tool and ensure Add To Selection is checked in the Options bar. Click in a few of the cells that will be the same color in the final piece.

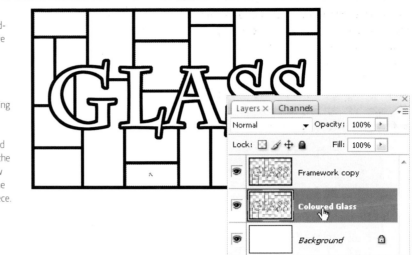

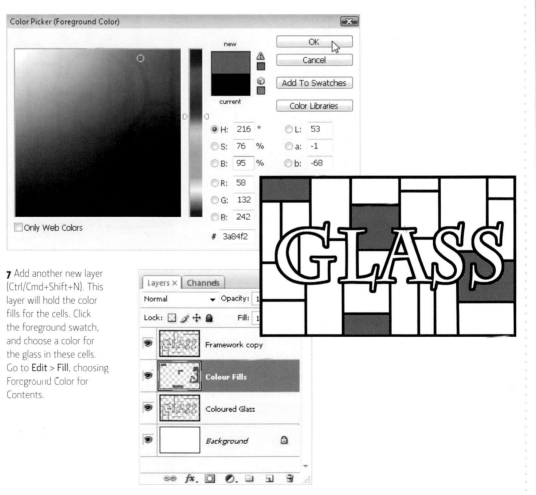

7 Add another new layer (Ctrl/Cmd+Shift+N). This layer will hold the color fills for the cells. Click the foreground swatch, and choose a color for the glass in these cells. Go to **Edit > Fill**, choosing Foreground Color for Contents.

Glass effect continued

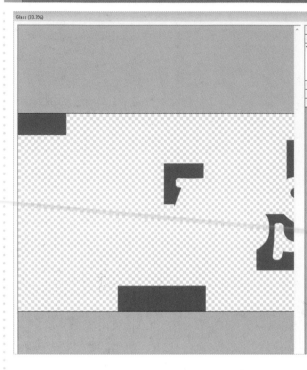

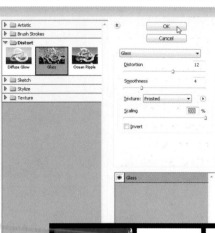

8 Now we'll apply the glass texture to these cells. With the selection still active, click on the Color Fills layer in the Layers palette and go to **Filter > Distort > Glass**.

Use 12 for distortion, 4 for Smoothness, 200% for Scale, and Frosted for Texture. Once the filter has been applied, hit Ctrl/Cmd+D to deselect.

Tip

TWILIGHT GLASS

As an alternative, and to create a stained glass effect with a much more atmospheric feel to it, try changing the blending mode of the top-most Color Fill layer to Difference and reducing the layer opacity a little.

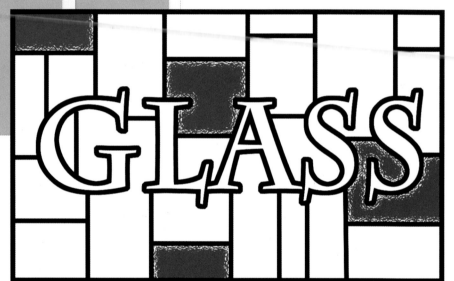

9 Repeat steps 6 to 8 to fill the other cells with different colors and apply the Glass filter. Make sure the Framework Copy layer is active while the selections are made, but fill and apply the Glass filter on the Color Fills layer. Feel free to experiment with the settings and apply different Glass textures in the Glass filter to vary the effect throughout the panel.

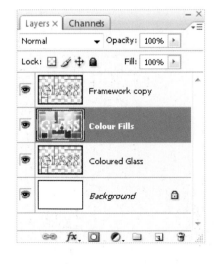

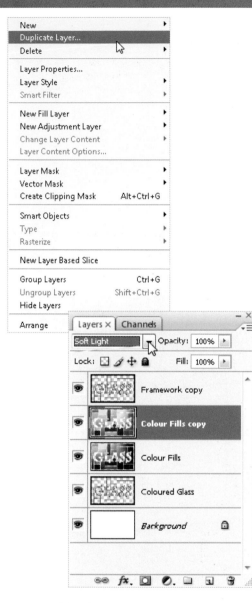

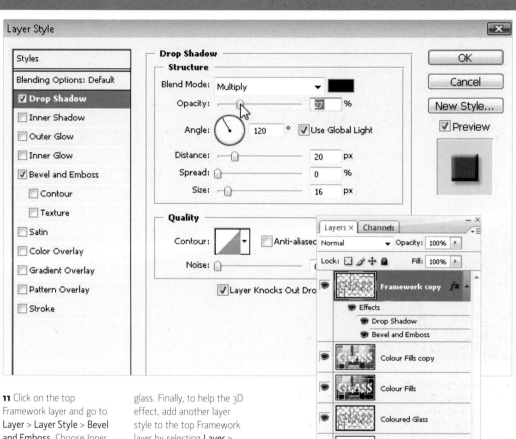

10 Once all of the cells are filled and filtered, duplicate the Color Fills layer by right-clicking/Ctrl-clicking it and selecting Duplicate Layer. Click on the lower of these two duplicate layers and go to **Filter > Render > Lighting Effects**. Use the default settings for the filter and drag the light pool to sit at the top left. Click OK and set the blending mode of the Color Fills copy layer to Soft Light.

11 Click on the top Framework layer and go to **Layer > Layer Style > Bevel and Emboss**. Choose Inner Bevel for Style, 161 for Depth, 16 for Size, and 7 for Soften. This will give the effect of heavy lead strips surrounding the pieces of glass. Finally, to help the 3D effect, add another layer style to the top Framework layer by selecting **Layer > Layer Style > Drop Shadow**. Set the opacity to 27%, Distance to 20, leave Spread on 0, and set Size to 16.

Plastic effect

You are probably familiar with the plastic effect that is often applied to display type or clickable buttons on web pages. While the effect applied to these objects is very effective, we'll try something different here, and apply it to a human hand. There's great potential for using this technique to create some weird and wonderful android and sci-fi images.

We'll use Photoshop's Plastic Wrap filter, combined with a few layer blending modes and styles, to create this unique effect.

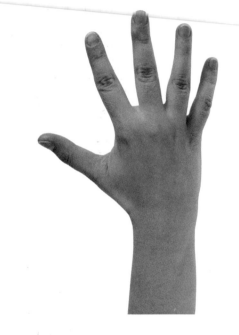

1 Here, we'll "plasticize" a hand. With the start image open, choose the Magic Wand tool and set the Tolerance to 10 in the Options bar. Click with the Wand in the white area around the hand. Invert the selection, using **Select > Inverse** (Ctrl/Cmd+Shift+I). Go to **Edit > Copy** (Ctrl/Cmd+C) and then go to **Edit > Paste** (Ctrl/Cmd+V) to paste the hand onto a new layer. Right-click/Ctrl-click this pasted layer and choose Duplicate Layer so we have two hand layers.

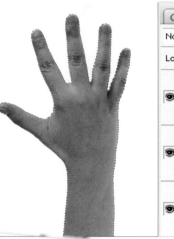

2 To begin the plastic effect, click on the upper hand layer and go to **Filter > Artistic > Plastic Wrap**. In the Plastic Wrap dialog box, select 12 for Highlight Strength, 1 for Detail, and 15 for Smoothness. Click OK to apply the filter. Now, drag this layer below the lower hand layer in the Layers palette and rename it "Plastic Wrap."

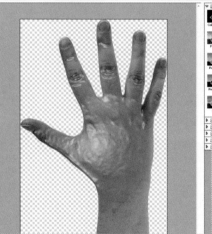

Tip

SUMPTUOUS STYLES!

With this effect, you're not limited to using the style you've used here. It's worth experimenting with many of the styles in the Web Styles library for the effect of different colored plastics and materials. Go on, try it. You might be pleasantly surprised!

3 Click on the top Hand layer. On this layer, we'll use a Photoshop style and make modifications to it. Display the Styles palette using **Window > Styles**. Click the small, right-pointing arrow in the Styles palette, choose Web Styles and click OK. From the Style thumbnails in the palette, choose Blue Gel With Drop Shadow. Don't worry if the effect doesn't look too realistic, as we'll modify it in the next step.

162

4 Set the blending mode for this layer to Darken, reducing the layer opacity to 75%. In the Layers palette, double-click the Hand layer to bring up the Layer Style dialog box, then double-click the words Bevel and Emboss. Change the Depth value to 71%, and the Size to 152. While the dialog box is still open, uncheck the box for Outer Glow, on the left.

5 Click on the Plastic Wrap layer and change its blending mode to Luminosity.

6 Now, click on the background layer and go to **Image > Adjustments > Hue and Saturation**. Grab the Hue slider and drag it to the left until the Hue value reads −131. This will give the hand an otherworldly blue color.

7 Finally, double-click the entry in the Effects panel on the top layer for Drop Shadow. Change the Distance value to 191 and the Size to 103.

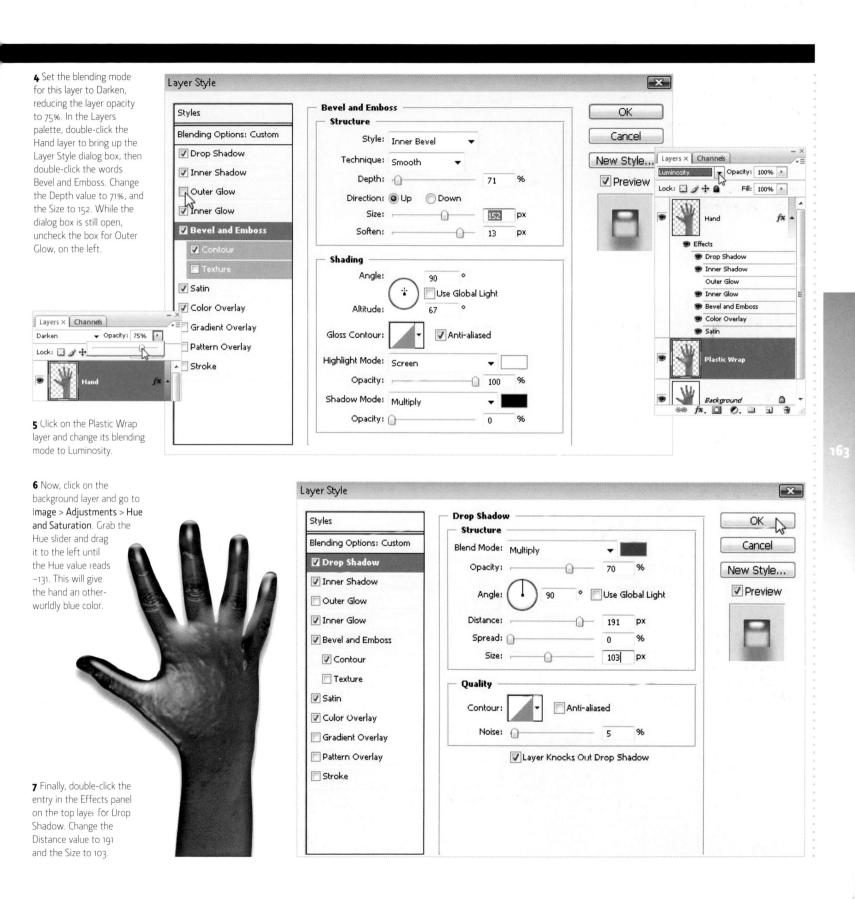

PRESENTATION EFFECTS

Frame effect
Vignette effects
Painterly borders
Out of the frame

Frame effect

Every great image deserves a great frame. With Photoshop at our disposal, we have the ability to frame images digitally with surprising ease. What's more, unlike a local framing shop, Photoshop offers an almost endless array of colors and textures to choose from.

Essentially, the frame is constructed of simple flat fills on a couple of layers, combined with the power of Photoshop styles. By using Bevel and Emboss layer styles, we can create realistic molded frames with strong textures and beautiful effects.

Try this easy recipe and don't just print those images – frame them!

1 Open the image to be framed in Photoshop. We need to extend the canvas to allow space around the image for the frame. Hit D on the keyboard to revert to default foreground/ background colors and go to **Image > Canvas Size**. Ensure that the measurement units are set to inches for Width and Height. Now, check the Relative checkbox. We want a fairly heavy frame on this image, so enter 2.5 inches in both the Width and Height boxes. Make sure that the central box is selected in the Anchor box and click OK.

2 Now, choose the Magic Wand tool from the Toolbar, set the Tolerance to 10 in the Options bar, and click in the white border to generate a selection. Add a new layer to the image (Ctrl/Cmd+Shift+N), naming it "Frame." Fill this selection using **Edit > Fill**, choosing White for fill Contents.

3 Hit Ctrl/Cmd+D on the keyboard to deselect. Now add another layer, naming it "Frame Trim." On this layer we'll create a thinner section running around the frame. Choose the Rectangular Marquee tool and, from the Options bar, choose Subtract from Selection. For guidance making the next selection, display the grid using **View > Show > Grid**.

4 Using the grid as a guide, drag a selection about halfway through the width of the frame surround.

5 Click and drag another selection a small distance inside the previous one, making a thin strip selection running around the frame. Fill this selection using **Edit > Fill**, choosing 50% Gray as the fill color. Hide the grid, using **View > Show > Grid**.

6 Now we need to give the frame a surface. Display the Styles palette, using **Window > Styles**. Click again on the Frame layer. In the Styles palette, click the small, right-pointing arrow and choose the Textures style set. From the Styles swatches, select Painted Wallboard.

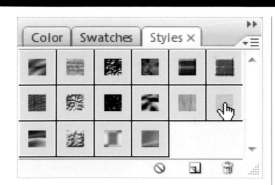

8 Return to the Frame Trim layer, and choose the Oak swatch from the Styles palette. Emboss this layer by going to **Layer > Layer Style > Bevel and Emboss**. Choose Pillow Emboss for Style and Smooth for Technique. Adjust the Depth, Size, and Soften sliders to taste. Click OK to apply the layer style.

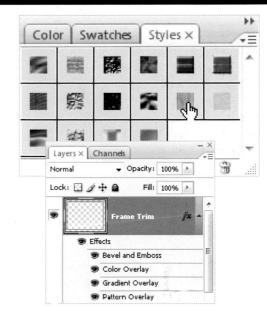

7 Now that the main frame is decorated, we need to give it a 3D look. Go to **Layer > Layer Style > Bevel and Emboss**. Choose Inner Bevel for Style and Chisel Hard for Technique. Set the Depth slider to 81, Size to 46, and Soften to 16. These sliders can be adjusted to increase or decrease the depth of the frame as desired. Click OK to apply the layer style.

Tip

MORE STYLES

There are many variations on this simple frame, which you can alter to your own tastes or to suit a particular image by simply choosing another style from the Styles palette. Photoshop has many textures and surfaces contained within the various style sets, which are available by clicking the small, right-pointing arrow in the palette.

167

Vignette effects

The vignette, another classic photographic printing technique, is presented here with a digital twist. In essence, a vignette (an edge effect in which the image fades off gradually) can be a soft mask of any shape around an image, and can be easily applied digitally with the aid of a simple layer mask. Layer masks are effective because we can construct any black-filled shape on a mask and use it as a vignette. The degree of blur for the shape is achieved using the Gaussian Blur filter. This gives us almost unlimited possibilities, and raises this classic technique to new heights.

168

1 For the vignette effect to be successful, the original image needs to have plenty of room around the main subject.

Begin by adding a new blank layer to the chosen image (Ctrl/Cmd+Shift+N) and calling it "Vignette."

3 Once the vignette selection is in position, choose an appropriate color for the fill by clicking the foreground color swatch.

Then, invert the selection by going to **Select > Inverse** (Ctrl/Cmd+Shift+I).

2 The simplest vignette is the classic oval. Choose the Elliptical Marquee tool from the Toolbar and ensure that Normal is selected from the Mode box in the Options bar. Drag an oval selection within the image, covering the center of interest. The selection can be moved into place by simply clicking and dragging inside the active selection.

4 To fill the vignette selection with the foreground color, choose the Paint Bucket tool and click within the active selection. After filling, hit Ctrl/Cmd+D on the keyboard to deselect.

5 Blur the vignette layer to create the effect. Go to **Filter > Blur > Gaussian Blur** and make sure that the Preview box is checked in the Gaussian Blur dialog box. The higher the blur radius setting, the softer the vignette effect will be, so experiment with the slider until a satisfactory result is reached. I've chosen a radius of about 41. Click OK.

7 Any of the other selection Marquee tools can be used to create the vignette, so it's worth experimenting with different shapes in the initial stages.

9 Click on the Paths palette tab and right-click/ Ctrl-click the Work Path, choosing Make Selection. Invert the selection, using **Select > Inverse** (Ctrl/ Cmd+Shift+I). Then fill and blur the vignette by the procedure detailed in the previous steps.

6 Tweak the color of the vignette layer using **Image > Adjustments > Hue/ Saturation**. Check the Preview box, and move the Hue slider to find an appealing color.

8 You can also use the Custom Shape tool to create the vignette. This gives a great deal of flexibility for creating the initial shape. After adding the new layer, choose the Custom Shape tool from the Toolbar. Ensure that the Paths icon is selected in the Options bar and choose a shape from the Shape Picker. Drag the shape over the image.

Painterly borders

It's surprising how a simple border effect can elevate a run-of-the-mill snapshot into a more attractive piece of art. Painterly borders in particular lend a certain sophistication to an image, and are surprisingly easy to create.

With Photoshop, half of the work is already done for us, as we have a vast selection of natural media and texture effect brushes at our fingertips. These special brushes are stored in brush libraries, which can be loaded from the Brush Picker using the small, right-pointing arrow. Again, layer masks are key to this technique, allowing us to achieve very subtle levels of varying opacities in the border.

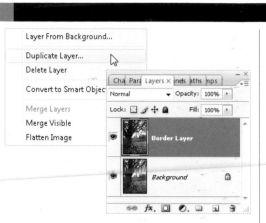

1 Open an appropriate image and right-click/Ctrl-click the background layer. Choose Duplicate Layer from the sub-menu, and name the new layer "Border Layer." This will form the main image layer that will have the border applied to it.

2 The original background layer will become the virtual canvas beneath the image layer. Click on the background layer. Choose two similar colors for the foreground and background at the bottom of the Toolbar, one slightly darker in tone than the other.

3 Hide the Border layer by clicking its visibility eye in the Layers palette. Click on the background layer and go to **Filter > Render > Clouds**. Blur it considerably with Gaussian Blur. I've used a radius setting of about 60. Rename this layer "Canvas" by double-clicking the background layer in the Layers palette.

4 Activate the Border layer again and go to **Edit > Transform > Scale**. Lock the Maintain Proportions link in the Options bar and reduce the size of the layer with the corner handles (the size of the window may need to be increased so that the handles can be seen clearly). When you're happy with the resizing, click the Commit checkmark in the Options bar.

Tip

IT'S BLACK AND WHITE

Remember that layer masks work on a purely grayscale basis, where white reveals the associated layer and black hides it. Shades of gray (or black at lower opacity) partially reveal the associated layer, so by using a pressure-sensitive stylus and tablet you can achieve very subtle transparency tricks around your border.

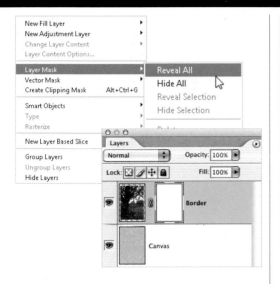

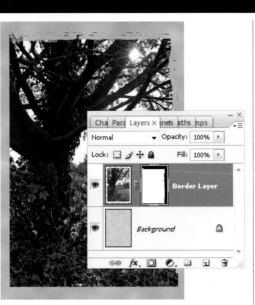

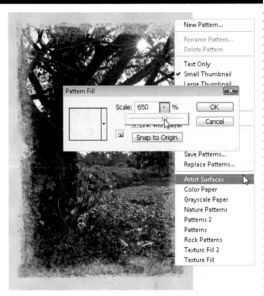

5 Add a layer mask to the Border layer, using **Layer > Layer Mask > Reveal All**.

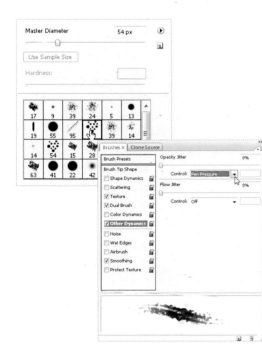

6 With the layer mask active, select the Brush tool and click in the Brush Picker. Click the right-pointing arrow and choose Wet Media Brushes. Load the brushes and select Rough Dry Brush from the thumbnails. If you're using a graphics tablet, hit F5 to display the Brush Options panel. Click the Other Dynamics category and set the Opacity Jitter control box to Pen Pressure. Ensure that the Shape Dynamics category is unchecked.

7 Increase the brush size, using the square bracket keys on the keyboard, and paint around the outside edge of the image, using black for the foreground color. Completely obliterate the edge, giving it a rough, broken effect.

8 Reselect the Brush Picker and choose Large Texture Stroke. Set Opacity Jitter to Pen Pressure if you're using a graphics tablet. Paint with black around the edge of the image, this time painting further inside the outer edge at a lower opacity to create semi-transparent brushstrokes. Reduce the opacity of the black the farther into the image you paint.

9 Finally, to add a touch of texture, select the Canvas layer in the Layers palette and click the "Create new fill or adjustment layer" icon at the base of the palette. Choose Pattern from the menu and click in the Pattern thumbnail. Load the Artist Surfaces and choose Canvas. Increase the pattern scale to 650 and click OK. Set the blending mode for this layer to Soft Light.

171

Out of the frame

By definition, frames and mounts are enclosing devices, but in the world of Photoshop anything is possible. Here, subject and frame interact; 2D melds with 3D, complete with the interplay of shadows. The key to this project is the stacking order of multiple layers; the use of a Bevel and Emboss layer style completes the illusion. This is a great technique for adding an extra dimension to images.

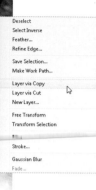

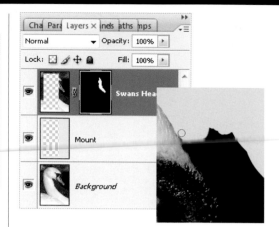

1 Open the image of the swan. Use the Rectangular Marquee tool to make an off-center selection, ensuring that the swan's beak and part of its head project outside the selection itself. Go to **Select** > **Inverse** (Ctrl/Cmd+Shift+I) and right-click/Ctrl-click within the selection, choosing Layer Via Copy.

3 Hit Ctrl/Cmd+D to deselect and click on the Swan's Head layer. Add a layer mask, using **Layer > Layer Mask > Reveal All**. Choose the Brush tool and paint black onto the mask to hide everything on the layer except the swan's head. Zoom in very close to mask around the outline of the head, using a very small brush. If you accidentally break into the head outline, swap the background and foreground colors and paint back into the mask with white. When it's complete, right-click/Ctrl-click the layer mask thumbnail and choose Apply Layer Mask.

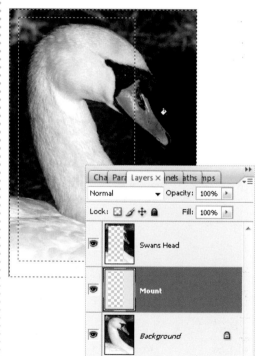

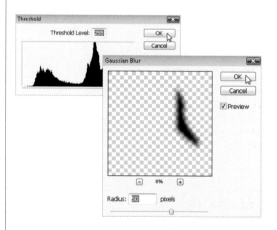

2 In the Layers palette, rename the new top layer "Swan's Head." Ctrl/Cmd-click this layer thumbnail to make a selection from its transparency. Then return to the background layer, add a new layer (Ctrl/Cmd+Shift+N), and call it "Mount." Choose a light straw color for the foreground and click inside the selection with the Bucket Fill tool.

4 Duplicate the Swan's head layer (Ctrl/Cmd+J) and go to **Image** > **Adjustments** > **Threshold**. Drag the pointer to the right to turn the layer element completely black and click OK. Now, blur the layer by going to **Filter** > **Blur** > **Gaussian Blur**, using a radius of 50 pixels.

5 Drag this layer below the layer containing the swan's head, reduce the opacity to 55% and set the blending mode to Darken. Go to **Edit** > **Transform** > **Scale** and drag the corner handles to enlarge the shadow a little. Before committing the transformation, move the shadow down and to the right a little. Erase any shadow that shows over the swan's head.

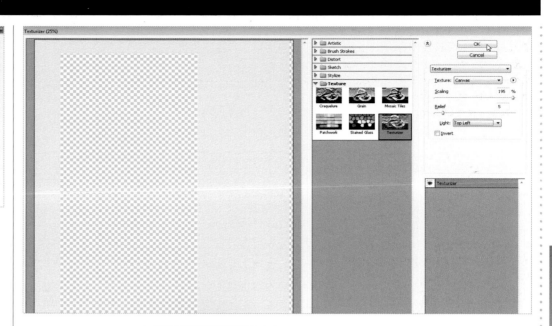

6 In the Layers palette, return to the Mount layer and click the "Add a layer style" button at the bottom of the palette, choosing Bevel and Emboss. In the dialog box, choose Inner Bevel for the Style and experiment with the Depth slider before clicking OK. I settled on a depth of 131.

8 Return to the Mount layer and go to **Filter** > **Texture** > **Texturizer**. Choose Canvas for the texture, use a high Scale value, and choose Top Left for Light Direction.

7 Click the background layer and choose a light cream color for the background color. Go to **Image** > **Canvas** Size, check the Relative box, and add one inch to each dimension.

173

9 Choose the Vertical Type tool, click on the Swan's head layer, and click in the image to add the text. Adjust the font and size, and select a suitable color, using the Options bar. Hit the Commit checkmark in the Options bar to fix the type.

Tip

CREATING AND MODIFYING TYPE

Using both the Horizontal and Vertical Type tool, there are many ways in which you can modify the appearance of the type itself. The size of the type and the font face can be chosen from the Options bar while the tool is active. A useful shortcut here is to click once in either of these options, and then use the up and down arrow keys on the keyboard to scroll through the various fonts and sizes. Many more variables can be found in the Character palette, displayed using Window > Character. Type can be re-edited at any point during the image-making process by double-clicking the thumbnail for the type layer in the Layers palette.

Glossary

Adjustment layer A specialized layer that can be handled as a conventional layer, but designed to enact effects on layers below it in the image "stack." These include changes to levels, contrast, and color, plus gradients and other effects. These changes do not permanently affect the pixels underneath, so by masking or removing the adjustment layer, you can easily remove the effect from part or all of an image with great ease. You can also return and change the parameters of an adjustment layer at a later stage.

Alpha channel A specific channel used to store transparency information. Alpha channels can be used to store and control selections and masks.

Blending mode In Photoshop, individual layers can be blended with those underneath, rather than simply overlaying them at full opacity. Blending modes control the ways in which the layers interact, enacting changes on one layer using the color information in the other. The result is a new color based on the original color and the nature of the blend.

Burn A method of locally darkening areas in a photograph. The opposite of Dodge.

Channels In Photoshop, a color image is usually composed of three or four separate single-color images, called channels. In standard RGB mode, the Red, Green, and Blue channels will each contain a monochromatic image representing the parts of the image that contain that color. In a CMYK image, the channels will be Cyan, Magenta, Yellow, and Black. Individual channels can be manipulated in much the same way as the composite image.

Color cast A bias in a color image, either intentionally introduced or the undesirable consequence of a mismatch between a camera's white balance and lighting. For example, tungsten lighting may create a warm yellow cast, or daylight scenes shot outdoors with the camera's color balance set for an indoor scene may have a cool blue cast.

Contrast The degree of difference between adjacent tones in an image, from the lightest to the darkest.

Crop To trim or mask an image so that it fits a given area or so that unwanted portions can be discarded.

Curves A Photoshop tool for precise control of tonal relationships, contrast, and color.

Depth of field The range in front of the lens in which objects will appear in clear focus. With a shallow depth of field, only objects at or very near the focal point will be in focus and foreground or background objects will be blurred. Depth of field can be manipulated in-camera for creative effect, and Photoshop CS2's new Lens Blur filter enables you to replicate it in postproduction.

Dodge A method of lightening areas in a photograph. The opposite of Burn.

Drag To move an item or selection across the screen, by clicking and holding the cursor over it, then moving the mouse with the button still pressed.

Eyedropper A tool used to define the foreground and background colors in the Tools palette, either by clicking on colors that appear in an image, or in a specific color palette dialog box. Eyedroppers are also used to sample colors for Levels, Curves, and Color Range processes.

Feather An option used to soften the edge of a selection that has been moved or otherwise manipulated, in order to hide the seams between the selected area and the pixels that surround it.

Fill A Photoshop operation which covers a defined area with a particular color, gradient, or texture pattern.

Gradient A gradual blend between two colors within a selection. The Gradient tool can be set to create several types, including linear, radial, and reflected gradients.

Graphics tablet A drawing device consisting of a stylus and a pressure-sensitive tablet. Many people find them easier to use than mice for drawing. The pressure sensitivity can be set to different functions, such as controlling the opacity of an eraser, or the width of a brush.

Grayscale An image or gradient made up of a series of 256 gray tones covering the entire gamut between black and white.

Halftone A technique of reproducing a continuous tone image on a printing press by breaking it up into a pattern of equally spaced dots of varying size—the larger the dots, the darker the shade.

Handle An icon used in an image-editing application to manipulate an effect or selection. These usually appear on screen as small black squares which can be moved by clicking and dragging with the mouse.

Hard light A blending mode that creates an effect similar to directing a bright light on the subject, emphasizing contrast and exaggerating highlights.

High-key image An image comprised predominantly of light tones.

Histogram A graphic representation of the distribution of brightness values in an image, normally ranging from black at the left-hand vertex to white at the right. Analysis of the shape of the histogram can be used to evaluate tonal range.

Lab Color mode An intermediate color mode used by Photoshop when converting from one mode to another. It is based on the CIE L*a*b* color model, where the image is split into three channels, "L," the luminance or lightness channel, and two chromatic components, "a" (green to red) and "b" (blue to yellow).

Layer A feature used to produce composite images by suspending image elements on separate overlays. Once these layers have been created, they can be re-ordered, blended, and their transparency (opacity) may be altered.

Layer styles A series of useful preset effects that can be applied to the contents of a layer. Examples include drop shadows, embossing, and color tone effects.

Layer mask A mask that can be applied to elements of an image in a particular layer, defining which pixels will or will not be visible or affect pixels underneath.

Levels A Photoshop tool that allows you to assess and adjust the tonal range of an image using a histogram. Can also be used to correct color casts.

Low-key image A photographic image consisting of predominantly dark tones, either as a result of lighting, processing, or digital image editing.

Midtones The range of tonal values that exist between the darkest and lightest tones in an image.

Motion blur In photography, the blurring effect caused by movement of objects within the frame during the exposure. Can be replicated using Photoshop filters.

Multiply A blending mode that uses the pixels of one layer to multiply those below. The resulting color is always darker, except where white appears on an upper layer.

Noise A random pattern of small spots on a digital image, usually caused by the inadequacies of digital camera CCDs in low-light conditions. Photoshop's Noise filters can add or remove noise from an image.

Opacity In a layered Photoshop document, the degree of transparency that each layer of an image has in relation to the layer beneath. As the opacity is lowered, the layer beneath shows through.

Overlay A blending mode that retains black and white in their original forms, but darkens dark areas and lightens light areas.

Pen tool A tool used for drawing vector paths in Photoshop.

PPI Pixels per inch. The most common unit of resolution, describing how many pixels are contained within a single linear inch of an image.

Quick Mask A feature designed to rapidly create a mask around a selection. By switching to Quick Mask mode, the user can paint and erase the mask using simple brushstrokes.

Resolution In digital images, the resolution is normally given as pixels per inch (PPI). Images for printing are usually 200-300ppi, and those for screen display, 72ppi.

Vanishing Point A new filter that allows you to warp images to a manually set perspective, either for cloning or 3D modelling.

Vector Path A shape (generated using paths) that is not pixel-dependant, so can be resized without a loss of quality.

174

Index

INDEX

Acknowledgments

Behind every good book, there's a great wife, and this one would have never happened without mine. Love you Bibs. x

Love and thanks to Mum and Dad for a life's worth of love, support, and constancy, and to Mum King for never losing faith. Many thanks also to Robert Townhill, Dennis and Kelly Kochanek, Paul and Sandra Fort, and everyone at the Priory at Grantham!

Thanks to everyone else who helped in any way with this project.

And finally, here's to absent friends.